For Alice, Dagmar, Dugald, Jay, Jerry and Sally

CHANGING THE WORLD IS THE ONLY FIT WORK FOR A GROWN MAN

*An eyewitness account of the life and times
of Howard Luck Gossage:
1960s America's most innovative, influential
and irreverent advertising genius*

STEVE HARRISON

Cover art and text designed by Jason King of King & Tuke
Typography and layout by Rachel Woodman and Adrian Sysum
Typeset in 12 on 17pt Centaur (of course)

CHANGING
THE WORLD
IS THE ONLY
FIT WORK
FOR A
GROWN MAN

WITHDRAWN

Other works by the author:

How to do better creative work
First published by Pearson Education Ltd in 2009

Contents

Foreword

"I told my daughter that I was coming here today, seeing somebody who wants to talk about Gossage and she said, 'Tell them what he told you.'
I said, 'Which one?'
And she said, 'You know, about what grown people do'.
And I remembered. He said, 'Changing the world is the only fit work for a grown man'."

Dugald Stermer

ACKNOWLEDGEMENTS

I suppose I should start by thanking Ogilvy & Mather Direct, New York – and then quickly apologising to them. Back in 1988, I'd been sent over there for a few weeks' work experience and, to further my education, was making use of the agency library. It was there that I saw *Is there any hope for advertising?* I'd never read anything like it, and was amazed to see that no one had taken the book out for 18 months. I immediately decided to "liberate" the book and put it to better use.

By that I mean it became my personal guide not just to writing ads, but to business life. Moreover, when I became creative director and then started my own agency, I insisted that everyone read *Is there any hope* ... and then *The Book of Gossage* when that came out in 1995.

One young beneficiary was an account executive called Ashley Pollak who, years later, filmed some of the interviews that inform this book. Another, way back in the early 'nineties, was Rory Sutherland. He became a lifelong Gossage fan, and has no doubt applied the things he learned from Gossage to the many important roles he's played within the Ogilvy organisation. If that is the case, then I hope the Ogilvy Group feel my original theft has been atoned for, and will think twice about levying the library fine.

Rory, along with Jeff Goodby, Rich Silverstein and Alex Bogusky have been generous in giving me their views on Howard Gossage's influence on them, the advertising industry and life in general. And I'd like to thank them for that.

However, my biggest debt of gratitude is owed to the "eyewitnesses" of this book's subtitle i.e. Howard Gossage's contemporaries.

I'll start with Alice Lowe. Just as she kept the Firehouse running, so she has helped steer this book to completion. Her contribution began with three fascinating interviews in San Francisco. She then paid me the huge compliment of giving me a copy of her unpublished biography of Howard Gossage. This has been an irreplaceable source of background detail, intelligent observation and rigorous analysis. Moreover, her writing style – at once economical and expressive – set a high bar for my own efforts. Speaking of which, throughout my writing of the book she has, with her usual good humour, been ever-ready to correct and cajole. Howard Gossage used to say "Give it to me straight, Al". And, in my case, she always has.

I must also make a point of thanking another woman who has kept the

Gossage flame burning for over forty years, *Advertising Age's* former European correspondent, Dagmar Mussey. Dagmar was the wife of Barrows Mussey who, whilst living in Germany, carried on a four year correspondence with his hero in San Francisco. Dagmar's friendship and encouragement have sustained me. As has her contribution for, as well as frequently suggesting new avenues of enquiry, she has given me complete access to all the Gossage-Mussey letters and, in so doing, allowed me to hear the authentic voice of Howard Gossage.

Alice's book and Dagmar's letters have been two of the three primary sources that have informed this book. Interviews with eyewitnesses have also been of immense importance. None more so than the occasions upon which I've been able to meet Sally Kemp. If Gossage was a showman who craved attention, then Sally was the perfect foil. And, despite her self-effacing protestations to the contrary, she shone as brightly as her husband, and guaranteed him the spotlight he craved. Her memory of him is still as strong as her love and respect for the man; and her initial interviews and subsequent emails have provided a unique insight into the private side of this most extrovert of men.

Of the other eyewitnesses I would like to thank Jerry Mander. Quite frankly I would not have been able to write Chapters 6 and 7 without him and, having heard his recollections, can only conclude that this hugely influential yet modest man deserves a biography dedicated to his story.

But then again, that's the thing about Howard Gossage. Everyone he was associated with was a larger-than-life talent and character. Dugald Stermer, who sadly died in December 2011, certainly fitted that description. His love of Gossage remained undimmed. As did his *joie de vivre* and charm. Of all the interviewees, it is easy to see why Gossage liked spending long lunches in Enrico's with Dugald Stermer. I bet they're up there now in the celestial branch, sharing a bottle of Paddy Irish Whiskey.

Jay Conrad Levinson was kind enough to get the whole research ball rolling by spending a cold October afternoon giving precious insight into the pre-Firehouse years of Weiner & Gossage. Nursing a bad head cold and operating to a merciless schedule, he would, I thought, give me 45 minutes. Three hours later, he was still going strong.

I'd have loved to interview the father of modern environmentalism, David Brower.

I got the next best thing with his son Kenneth who, in his own right, has done so much for the cause that — were he British — he'd undoubtedly be "Sir Ken". I was also fortunate enough to interview Tom Turner who was David Brower's assistant during most of the turbulent times described in Chapter 6. Both Ken and Tom spoke with a quiet intelligence and integrity, and left me feeling that these are the kind of Americans they don't make any more.

Apart, that is, from Professor Fred Turner of Stanford University, who invited me to his home to share his expertise on — as the title of his brilliant book suggests — everything from counterculture to cyberculture. I was doubly lucky because I was also invited round to James Harkin's home to develop those themes, with specific reference to Marshall McLuhan. Both men make pattern recognition look easy — as well as nice cups of tea.

Professor Greg Pabst took me to an ice cream parlour to share his views on Howard Gossage. And I'm much obliged, because it was Greg who provided me with the breakthrough thought that Gossage was building communities and developing a rudimentary form of social media 40 years before anyone else.

That's the kind of insight that would appeal to Dr. Hubert Burda who, amongst his many philanthropic pursuits, likes to explore the connection between technological innovation and social change. He was certainly philanthropic with me — putting the running of one of Europe's biggest publishing houses on hold for sixty minutes while he shared memories of his time with Howard Gossage.

In fact, I've been struck by the willingness of all my interviewees to make the time to talk to me. And I think this in itself is evidence of the hold that Howard Gossage still has on the people he encountered fifty years ago. That comes shining through the testimony given by Bob Scheer who was so eager to share his memories of Gossage that he insisted on talking even as he was travelling from the airport to a conference on the San Francisco BART. Similarly, Arthur Finger was so keen to help that he actually 'phoned me so I didn't have to pick up the cost of the long distance calls to Vancouver. Finally there was Bob McLaren who, just five days before I went to print, got in touch from Monte Carlo with not only his unique recollections but also a package of Gossage speeches, articles and the most personal of letters.

Suffice to say, the contributions of all three men were priceless.

All the people above have provided the content for this book. My efforts to order and arrange it properly have been aided by the following individuals.

Simon Tuke took on the thankless task of reacquainting me with the correct use of the hyphen, and the comma. He also tried to correct my typos, my spelling – and my carelessness when, for example, he pointed out that Anguilla's economy was not sustained by remittances from people who used to love the country but had gone off it (ex-patriots), but by people who were born there but had moved away (expatriates). If you still see mistakes then, sorry Simon, they are my fault and not yours.

His partner at the London agency King & Tuke is Jason King, and it is he who, with his assistant Emmeline Abolian, kindly worked as art director and typographer on this book. All the good things about the design and lay-out are the result of his skill, hard work and attention to detail. If there are any flaws then they are down to me not being clear enough with my publisher. Speaking of whom, I'd like to thank Miles Bailey and his colleagues Rachel and Adrian for their patience, advice and expertise.

As for what the book says, I'd like to thank Jon Steel who read the ten page treatment and insisted I continue; Jeremy Bullmore who, as a contemporary of Gossage, alerted me to the fact that this master of PR wasn't above the occasional bit of self-serving hyperbole; and Dr. Sean Dennis Cashman who pointed out the broader historical perspective.

Then there is Rory Sutherland who read it twice and then made the unusual request that I actually write more. And Andrew Cracknell who took the time to read the manuscript straight off his screen whilst bobbing around in his yacht in the Eastern Med. Not surprisingly under those circumstances, he suggested I write less. I also want to thank Stephen Timms for giving me access to his incredible library, and I must single out Tim Connor who has seen the manuscript develop and, more than anyone else, has provided clear direction, and concise criticism and comment about what needs elaborating upon and what needs eliding.

I say more than anyone else, but that isn't true. For, over the past 12 months, Morag Brennan has read the manuscript almost as many times as me, and on each occasion has pointed out where it is going wrong and how I might put it right. Her powers of perception are only exceeded by her patience, for she has lived with me and Howard Gossage 24 hours a day, seven days a week, and has been the fount of encouragement, ideas and good humour throughout.

Finally I'd like to thank Bruce Bendinger and Patrick Aylward for locating, scanning and sending over all the advertisements that you'll see here. If you want to read Gossage's own views on advertising, as encapsulated in his speeches and articles, then Barrows Mussey's book, and Bruce's extended appreciation, remain your first ports of call. What I've tried to do is explain who Howard Luck Gossage was, what he did and why he did it, using the testimony of those who knew, lived and worked with him. I hope I've done justice to them – and him.

LIST OF
ILLUSTRATIONS

IT'S A MAD, MAD, MAD, MAD WORLD

"ADVERTISING IS
A MULTI-BILLION
DOLLAR
SLEDGEHAMMER
DRIVING
A 49-CENT,
ECONOMY-SIZE
THUMBTACK"

On 12 October, 1962, *Time* magazine ran a cover featuring the faces of 12 white, middle-aged men. Look at them today and you'd think they were Wall Street bankers, Washington bureaucrats or character actors auditioning for a part as the strait-laced boss in some wholesome family series like *Bewitched* or *The Lucy Show*.

Turn, however, to the story inside and you'll see these were the original Mad Men – the slick suits who, either side of their three-Martini lunches, controlled America's advertising industry.

And what control they seemed to have. According to J.K. Galbraith's *The Affluent Society* (1958), they were manipulating and moulding the public's morals and mores in a manner never before seen in a democratic society. Worse still, if you were to believe that other totemic bestseller, Vance Packard's *The Hidden Persuaders* (1957), they were doing all this without anyone knowing it was happening.

According to Packard, their psychographic segmenters, psycholinguists, subliminal communicators, operant conditioners, psychometric specialists and message compression technologists were deviously tinkering with the tastes and appetites of a voracious consumer society.

It seemed there was a lot of money to be made out of such borderline mendacity. In 1957, the year *The Hidden Persuaders* was published, four agencies were posting well over $200 million a year in billings: J. Walter Thompson; McCann-Erickson; Young & Rubicam; and Batten, Barton, Durstine & Osborn (BBDO).[1]

And there was plenty left for the other agencies that lined that one-mile stretch of mid-town Manhattan between 200 and 650 Madison Avenue. Especially when you realise that General Motors, Procter & Gamble, Ford, General Foods and General Electric alone were allocating half a billion dollars a year to their advertising budgets.[2]

How to influence people – and lose friends

Yet as the 'fifties closed and the agencies contemplated an ever more lucrative future, they must have realised that their wealth and influence didn't translate into affection and respect. Indeed, there was a growing demand for books (both fiction and non) that chronicled the shortcomings of the advertising executive.

One of them, James Kelly's *The Insider* (1958), spoke in racy tones of "Madmen. The Mad League where everybody in America either pitches or catches, no matter how hard he denies it .... An ugly place when you're down and out; a thing of beauty when you're riding high."[3]

One of Kelly's "Madmen", Jim Ellis, alluded to such excesses in the introduction to his memoirs, "If you want to write a bestseller about the advertising business, the surest way is to turn the spotlight on one little corner of the business in which case you can portray it as a racket or a rat race – a racket in which you 'succeed without really trying' or you hypnotize people into buying things by the black art of using 'hidden persuaders' – or a rat race conducted by harassed hucksters, flirting with ulcers and coronaries, busily cutting each others' throats in the canyons of Madison Avenue."[4]

While Ellis went on to take a more reasoned view of the industry, even he would have admitted that advertising could itself have benefited from a spot of re-branding. Unfortunately, few at the time could be bothered improving the industry's image. There was, quite frankly, too much money to be made.

As the decade closed, that money carried on rolling in. As Whit Hobbs of Batten, Barton, Durstine & Osborn said in 1959, "We have lived through nearly all the Fabulous Fifties – the decade of the super highway and the supermarket, the family room and the TV dinner. The sky used to be the limit ... but suddenly there isn't any limit. We can no longer even conceive what the limit might be."[5]

Complicity, complacency and contentment

For the American public, the "Fabulous Fifties" were just that. They'd emerged from World War II breathing a huge sigh of relief that their great sacrifice had saved the world from the twin tyrannies of Nazism and Japanese Imperialism. Not only that, the Great Depression's soup kitchens, that everyone had expected to return once the munitions factories closed, miraculously never materialised.

It was a miracle born of a boom in construction and consumer goods married to cheap credit, and an automobile-driven dash to the suburbs. Never before had so many people enjoyed such material comfort. By the mid-'fifties their sigh of relief had turned into a long purr of contentment. At the decade's end, however, a growing number of social commentators led by William H. Whyte (*The Organisation Man*, 1956) and Norman Mailer (*The White Negro* in *Advertisements for Myself*, 1959) thought it sounded more like the snores of complacency.

In truth, despite the sensationalism of Packard's *The Hidden Persuaders*, these people weren't being manipulated any more than they wanted to be. After generations spent delaying gratification until the grim reaper showed up, they were simply enjoying the sanctioned self-indulgence of an affluent society founded on euphoric mass consumption.

As we'll see, their children would rail against the conformity and commercialism that was bred by such consumerism. But back to the 'fifties, and the cash papered over the cracks in society while the Mad Men dined out on their influence and toasted each other across the crowded tables at their expense-account hangouts.

Not a Mad Man, just angry

One agency chief, however, was refusing to raise his glass. For him the industry's claims were bogus. In fact, he likened the true impact of its efforts to "a multi-billion dollar sledgehammer driving a 49-cent, economy-size thumbtack".[6]

This was one adman who had no use for Packard's manipulative messaging or mesmerising techniques. His chosen method was the written word. Nor was he interested in the multi-million dollar budgets that were needed to drive the sinus-draining and pain-killing properties of Dristan and Anacin into the consumer's head via incessant, intrusive TV advertising. He preferred to do things differently.

Indeed, he'd rejected the strict hierarchies and loose morals of Madison Avenue's organisation men. To find him you'd have had to travel 3,000 miles across the USA to that advertising backwater, San Francisco. And you'd have had to look pretty hard because his agency never totalled more than 13 people.

Yet out of the Firehouse on 451 Pacific Avenue came interactive advertising, cause-related marketing and PR-generating campaigns that were forty years ahead of their time. To those who'd listen, he was also bandying around ideas about Pay per View, and stand-alone specialist media buying agencies decades before the former revolutionised TV broadcasting and the latter transformed the advertising industry.

Important though such innovations are to those who work in the media, his influence was much greater than that. For it is to his agency that we can trace the roots of two of the most important phenomena of the late 20th and early 21st Centuries: social media and the Green Movement.

This man's name was Howard Luck Gossage. No, he was never a Mad Man, but when he saw the world that the Mad Men's ads were creating, he was often very angry. And he was determined to change it. Not by emulating his industry peers, but by looking beyond advertising to the galvanising ideas of his age – and harnessing them.

This is the story of his life and times.

Chapter 1

THE MOST UNEMPLOYABLE PERSON I KNOW

"IN BAITING
A TRAP WITH CHEESE,
ALWAYS LEAVE ROOM
FOR THE MOUSE"

Some of you who are reading this, especially those who don't work in advertising, may have had your interest piqued by the TV series *Mad Men*. If so, you should know right now that Howard Luck Gossage was not one of those people. Indeed, his wife Sally Kemp, gets very annoyed when asked "is the show about Howard?"[1]

Yet Sally would happily concede that Gossage was like his TV counterparts in one particular way. He looked, in every inch of his lean, six-foot frame, like a leading man.

His colleague, art director Dugald Stermer, certainly thought so. As he explains, "His complexion was corpse-like, porcelain. He looked older than his age ... his hair was absolutely white and I don't know how he did it but it always looked flowing but was always in one place. He was a great-looking guy. He was very dramatic-looking. Looked more like an actor than an advertising man."[2]

Sally Kemp was a beautiful Broadway actress when they met and, as such, was used to the company of great-looking leading men. Yet, as she recalls, "When I first saw him I thought 'Oh my, I would give *anything* to be meeting a man like that.'"[3] That's quite a reaction when you realise that Sally had only recently spurned the advances of Richard Burton who, in those pre-Liz and booze days, had been tagged the world's most desirable man.

Gossage's right-hand woman at the agency, Alice Lowe, was also impressed: "He had an imperious nose, saved from disdainful hauteur by an unexpectedly bashed-in tip. A wide expressive mouth, ready to break into a broad conspiratorial grin at the slightest provocation, betrayed an innate puckishness. An exceptionally pale, luminous complexion added a suggestion of mystery; it lit his lined, craggy face with a faint, pearly sheen, as if an imaginative, omnipotent Stage Manager had decreed that a soft light be focused on Gossage and then provided Howard with a perpetual spotlight of his own."[4]

That spotlight was well placed. For, as Alice explained, "There is no question that Howard was every bit as much an actor as Sally."[5] And one who fully understood the significance of the Latin inscription painted in gilt on the wooden frame of the massive antique mirror that stood in his agency's conference room: "Do not look into this mirror to see yourself as you are, but as you would like to be, and you will become that desired image."[6]

Jerry Mander, the only copywriter who Gossage ever felt understood him, also saw the actor in the adman. To Mander, Gossage was "a ham. He occupied the room. If he was to walk into a room, all eyes would turn to him."[7]

By all accounts, this pleased Gossage greatly. As we'll see, he needed an audience simply to get him excited about the day that lay ahead of him. For Gossage divided mankind into two types: "Mammonoids", who are motivated by money, and "Tediophobes", who hate tedium; and he was firmly in the latter camp. Easily bored, he was in constant search of the company of others and the stimulation of intelligent, interesting conversation.

A lonely boy's search for attention

Staving off boredom was one motivation. There was, however, a deeper-seated reason for his need for an audience. As his wife Sally surmised, it was to compensate for the love that was absent in childhood.

Howard's mother, Alice, was one in a long line of vaudevillians, and was away on tour for ten months of the year. The boy doted on her and was dismayed when, in her absence, he had to stay with either his grandparents or his father, Clyde. The indifference was mutual and Clyde's coldness only accentuated his longing for his mother's affection. It also had another lasting effect. One day, having broken a toy, the four year old Howard was so fearful of his father's reaction that he developed the stammer that would stay with him for the rest of his life.

To make matters worse, the lonely boy was prevented from forming lasting friendships by a peripatetic childhood and youth that took him and his sister, Jane, from Chicago to New York, Denver, New Orleans, Kansas City and finally Houston. In the Depression-racked 1930s such wanderings were the prerogative of the dispossessed, and Howard was aware of the stigma. As he said later, "I seem to have spent most of my teen years at least being ashamed of something or another; the smell of poverty, inadequacy and social unacceptability."[8]

His marginalisation was exaggerated by an un-American aversion to team games and sport which distanced him even further from his young peers and, in turn, reinforced the longing for company and attention that would so inform his personal and professional life.

From hick to Huck

When he enrolled at Kansas City University, the 18 year old Gossage was a lonely hick from the sticks and very far removed from the urbane "boule-vardier" and "man of the world" who, as we'll see, so impressed journalists Tom Wolfe and Bob Scheer.[9] Whence the transition? Well, maybe it's not too fanciful to trace it to his reading and re-enactment of a scene from the life of that other Midwestern outsider, Huckleberry Finn. In that scene Huck dispenses with an inconvenient persona by faking his own death and heading off down the Mississippi. Suitably inspired, Gossage persuaded a friend to accompany him on a similar excursion.*

The 1500-mile journey took six weeks. For a dreadful athlete and someone who throughout their life had a Transylvanian aristocrat's aversion to direct sunlight, this was an arduous adventure. But it left him with much more than calloused hands and a weather-beaten face for, as he negotiated the Mississippi currents, he got his first lesson in manipulating the media.

At every stop along the way, he called into the local newspaper office or radio station to report his progress. Ever hungry for news, the editors picked up the story and quickly the trip was transformed from a madcap jaunt into a media-event that turned the two boys into minor celebrities.

In years to come Gossage would organise a similar journey from San Francisco to Seattle. As we'll see, it would be the focus of a much larger media circus and conse-quently a huge commercial success for its backer, Rainier Ale.

If the Mississippi canoe trip was the prototype for that campaign and many others, then it was also a rite of passage for its author. He kept the newspaper cuttings for the rest of his life and, as Alice Lowe reported, "When asked in later years to

*There are close parallels between Gossage's life and career and those of the British advertising man, David Ogilvy. Both were lonely, unloved little boys who saw in Huck Finn's untroubled free spirit a prototype for the autonomous, adventurous hero they sought to become. As Ogilvy said, Huckleberry Finn "possessed my soul to such an extent that I decided to light out for the Mississippi at the first opportunity."[10] In his biography of Ogilvy, Ken Roman makes it clear that childhood insecurity had the same effect on the adult Ogilvy as it had on Gossage: an actor's need for the spotlight. What Roman writes of one could easily be applied to the other, "To understand the man, one has to grasp first that Ogilvy was an actor."[11]

When asked to list the things of which he was most proud, Gossage always mentioned his canoe trip as his first major accomplishment. The second? With a wry grin he usually answered: "Marrying my third wife, Sally Kemp." Here she is in a publicity still taken by Firehouse photographer, George Dipple.

list the achievements he was proud of, Gossage always mentioned his canoe ride as his first major accomplishment. The second? With a wry grin, the answer usually was, 'Marrying my third wife, Sally Kemp'."[12]

The power of the written word and the USAF bomber

It was also at Kansas City University that Gossage realised he could get an audience through his writing and, in 1937, became a joint-founder of and contributor to the college humour magazine, *The Kangaroo*.

Moreover, it was whilst working on *The Kangaroo* that Gossage learned the power of the well-written, audacious letter. The publication needed a cover design and, with what would become typical chutzpah, Gossage decided that the best person to provide it would be Walt Disney. The letter went out and, against everyone's expectation, the movie mogul sent back the drawing, free of charge.

In future, Gossage would write to anyone, regardless of fame or fortune, if and when the mood took him. For example, in 1952, whilst travelling in Europe he wrote to his great hero, Bertrand Russell, and asked if he could visit him in Cambridge. Thereafter, one of his most treasured possessions was a signed and framed type-written quote from the mathematician and philosopher. A few years later, Gossage also wrote to the Nobel Prize winning novelist John Steinbeck and thus started a long and very close friendship. Finally, as we'll see in his approach to Marshall McLuhan, if Gossage was particularly inspired to get in touch then the letter would be preceded by a direct 'phone call.

All of that lay in the future. Standing immediately between college kid Gossage and what was ultimately to be a career in advertising was the not inconsiderable obstacle known generally as World War II.

Gossage managed to negotiate the worst calamity in the world's history reasonably unscathed, and emerged as a hero – with two Distinguished Flying Crosses; and as a husband – with a wife, Frances Page Fox.

Lieutenant Gossage rarely spoke of his exploits as a pilot in the South Pacific Bomber Squadrons VB-104 and VB-119. When he did discuss winning the second of his Distinguished Flying Crosses he said he got it for peeing into a tube without spilling a drop whilst under prolonged Japanese anti-aircraft fire. His colleagues were thankful for that, and for his never having lost a fellow flyer on any of his missions. He was also renowned for his coolness, not least for one daredevil flight at just 25 feet above the waters of enemy-occupied Hong Kong harbour.

Howard Gossage returned from WWII a hero, with two Distinguished Flying Crosses.

Feeding the starving ...

Upon discharge, his intention was to enter the diplomatic corps. Thankfully, given his refusal to toe any kind of party-line, the international incident that this plan would probably have provoked was averted by Gossage's inability to master the basics of a foreign language.

Unsure what to do next, he landed a job as promotion manager at KLX radio station in Oakland, California. This entailed coming up with gimmicks and stunts aimed at getting local companies to advertise with the station.

One of his first ideas was the "balloon in a box" trick. Anyone who has worked in sales promotion or direct marketing will have hit upon this one fairly early in their careers. The idea is to put a helium-filled balloon in a box and then post it to your target in the hope that they'll be pleasantly surprised to see the balloon float upwards and outwards once the package is opened.*

Gossage quickly came up with better ideas. He also started to write advertisements for the station and was interested enough in copywriting to enlist in night school classes. At this time he also displayed another indication of the understanding of PR that distinguished his career, and signs of the altruism that ultimately transformed it.

It was 1949 and, while the US post-war economic boom was roaring ahead, much of Europe remained in ruins. Alongside his boss, Joe Connor, Gossage organised a party for Oakland's children, admission to which was a can of food. This food would then be collected, packaged and sent to France. When only a handful of kids turned up, Connor and the event's sponsors were dismayed. Gossage, however, was defiant. "Reality has nothing to do with it," he argued. "We will make this one of the most successful propaganda events ever. Reality is not what happens but is controlled by what is written and said about it. We control the print and the air. Remember all those starving French kids . . . ."[14]

The following day, the *Oakland Tribune* announced the party's success and informed all those unfortunate enough not to have shared in the event that they could still play a small part by leaving their cans of food at their local grocers ready for collection by the event's sponsor.

The cans rolled in, a plane was donated by one of the international carriers and Gossage was invited to accompany the mercy mission to Paris. He agreed – even though he knew that KLX would fire him for taking unauthorised leave.

Fire him they did. But Gossage wasn't too concerned. He'd been unable to resist the spotlight, and he quickly got another job at CBS. Moreover, at that time he was far from convinced that this line of work was for him. Indeed, doubts persisted and, in 1951, he took advantage of the wonderful munificence of the G.I. Bill of Rights

---

*A great practical joker, Gossage would take inspiration from the "balloon in a box trick". As his neighbour Arthur Finger explains, "Howard had bought a huge weather balloon from the local surplus store and invited someone from our block over for drinks and a game of chess. While they were distracted, he got into their apartment and inflated the balloon so it filled every inch of the place. He then returned to the party but couldn't wait to see how his guest would react when they returned home and opened their front door." [13]

and enrolled with the University of Geneva and the Sorbonne with the intention of getting a doctorate in history.

As Sally Kemp suggests, the real stimulus was the urge to travel, and he wasn't really cut out for academia. She's right, for as we'll see, Gossage's mind tended to be on fast spin as his attention whirled from subject to subject. There was certainly little in the older man that suggested he might have had the patience to spend years researching and writing the single line of argument that constitutes a doctoral thesis. The "Tediophobe" within him couldn't have stood it.

… and going hungry

True enough, in late 1953 he was back in San Francisco looking for a job in the only industry that had ever paid him a regular wage, advertising.

When, in December, he met Alice Lowe for the first time, he cut a forlorn figure. Alice was working as assistant to the PR manager for an agency owned by account executive, Joe Weiner. Gossage had come for an interview as a copywriter and, while impressing Weiner, had been rejected because of his lack of experience.

As Alice left the office for the day she encountered the crestfallen Gossage and accompanied him down Montgomery Street trying her best to lift his spirits. There was good reason for him to be down. He hadn't had a regular job for nearly three years. He was 36 years of age and struggling to make a home for his second wife while trying to keep up the alimony payments to his first wife and their five year old daughter.

When, on the corner of Montgomery and Market Street, Gossage disappeared into the evening gloom, he faced a grim Christmas, and a new year that promised only a long trawl round the other agencies in the advertising backwater that was San Francisco.

As Alice Lowe recalls, "He was kind of lost. He didn't know exactly what he wanted to do. He wasn't especially qualified for any particular thing and he knew that. He knew he was very bright in a general sort of way, but how do you apply that to everyday life?"[15]

Looking back, he gave this as some sort of answer, "What's so great about being a creative man? I don't think most of us have any choice about it. We took a flyer at several more legitimate things, and flunked out, before we ran into this peculiar thing that just happened to fit our bizarre talents."[16]

In Gossage's case, that bizarre talent finally found a place to flourish when, some weeks after his unsuccessful interview with Weiner, he joined the small San Francisco agency, Brisacher, Wheeler & Staff.

Making a name for himself – and Qantas

One of the first campaigns to showcase what was to become his customary style was created for Qantas, the Australian airline. The advertisement was originally intended to announce the news that Qantas now had its own Super Constellation aircraft for those seeking trans-oceanic and intercontinental travel. What they got from Gossage was far removed from the exercise in corporate chest-beating that they'd probably been expecting.

In a style of advertising that perfectly captured the irreverent, "no worries" brand essence of what we today describe as "Australianness", Gossage offered an unusual first prize to the person who could come up with a suitably striking name for Qantas's new Super Constellation airliner. His headline read, "Be the first one in your block to win a kangaroo!"

It was a style of advertising that typified its author's work. For Gossage's aim was always to involve the audience by enticing them in to play their part. As he summed it up, "In baiting a trap with cheese, always leave room for the mouse."[17]

Thousands of readers of *The New Yorker* magazine took the bait and, as a reward for their entries, received a badge which read "I Did It". Even in those relatively innocent, innuendo-free times, such a claim raised more than the occasional eyebrow at the office, country club and cocktail party.

Those anxious to know if they'd actually "Won It" waited a couple of weeks until another advertisement appeared in *The New Yorker* which announced: "New York child wins kangaroo, her first!" The lucky recipient turned out to be a little girl, Dena Siebert, from Stuyvesant Town, who'd thought it might be a good idea to call the plane "Sam".

The other big winner was Gossage.

Those two advertisements established him as a rising star of the West Coast

TWA SUPER-G Constellation

QANTAS SUPER- ? Constellation

BE THE FIRST ONE IN YOUR BLOCK TO WIN A KANGAROO!

WE ARE pleased as Punch with TWA, and we are sure that Henry Dreyfuss is, too. For TWA have chosen for their domestic service the same splendid *super* Super Constellation that Qantas flies across the world to 26 countries on 5 continents. Dreyfuss designed interior and all.

And we admire the special name TWA have chosen for their version of this ultra Super Constellation. Super-G just, well, *fits* as a designation. We wouldn't mind using it ourselves, seeing they've done such a bang-up job of advertising it, but would that be playing the game?

What we really want is a name of our *own*, neat, evocative, alluring; a name calculated to send hordes of tourists to their Travel Agents. Tourists brandishing fistfuls of large notes and

demanding to be sent via Qantas Super Constellation to Sydney, London, Johannesburg, Tokyo, or wherever. Wallowing in Henry Dreyfuss luxury at several hundred miles an hour. We need a name, and *your help.*

So we will be much obliged if you will fill out the attached entry blank and send it to us. Neatness and legibility will count for next to nothing, but please try to spell Qantas without a "u". You pronounce it* but you don't write it.

First prize is a real, live Kangaroo; second prize is a stuffed Koala Bear (*live* koala bears are very picky eaters — you wouldn't want one); and 98 prizes of one boomerang each. In addition, *every entrant* will receive, absolutely free, an explanation of why there is no "u" in Qantas. All set?

NEXT WEEK . . . *an idyllic domestic scene!*

*As in Qality.

OFFICIAL ENTRY BLANK

QANTAS
Union Square, San Francisco, California

MENIIII

I think it is a shame that your speedy, sybaritic Super Constellations do not have as nice a name as TWA's. In an effort to correct all this, I suggest that they be called:

AUSTRALIA'S OVERSEAS AIRLINE

NAME

ADDRESS

When Qantas asked for an ad announcing that they now had the Super Constellation aircraft they probably expected a piece of corporate chest-beating. Instead Gossage perfectly captured the irreverent, "no worries" brand essence of what we today describe as "Australianness".

NEW YORK CHILD WINS KANGAROO, HER FIRST!

THE gigantic Qantas Super Constellation naming contest is history and things just couldn't have worked out better, about the winning name we mean. It's got everything: class, verve, brevity! Especially brevity and class. And when you come right down to it, there's too much verve in the world today anyway, we say.

We won't keep you on tenterhooks any longer, the name is SAM! Not "Super Sam Constellation," just plain old Sam. And don't try to read any hidden meaning into the letters S-A-M, for it's no use. Sam. Oh, there's consternation at TWA tonight you can wager.

Of course there *may* be a little difficulty working this gracefully into our advertising. (Fly Qantas to the South Seas, Australia, the Far East, South Africa; or conversely from London to Rome, Cairo, Singapore, and around that way. All by Sam, splendid, speedy, Henry Dreyfuss-decorated Sam.) We'll think of something. If you think of something first please feel free to write. We insist on it, if it comes to that.

So, to you, Dena Walker Seibert, small daughter of Mr. and Mrs. Wilson Seibert, 17 Stuyvesant Oval, New York 9, N. Y., our Grand Prize Kangaroo and gratitude. Good show.

Now, in the travel trade category Norma Davis of the San Jose (Calif.) Travel Service wins a kangaroo as well. There'll be hopping in the streets of San Jose, one feels sure. And a kangaroo to Mr. Warren Lee Pearson, Chairman of the Board of TWA, so they can start their own contest. We personally feel that they're stuck with "Super G," though. After we started our contest, they were nice enough to say we could use "Super G" if we wanted to. Well, maybe we will from time to time, if it just happens to fit. And they can use Sam.

If you're wondering why all the kangaroos, the fact is we got carried away. And after all, it's that first kangaroo that's tough; the ones after that come easy. Winners of didjireedoos, stuffed koala bears, Qantas ties, and boomerangs will be told by mail. Congratulations, all!

Well, there are probably some die-hards around who think that Sam is an absolutely terrible name. Although we're a big corporation (ltd., but not very) we're willing to listen. We're not querulous*, so if you want to toss in your two bob's worth, pro or con, even at this late date, go on ahead. A simple "Sam!" or "Sam?" scrawled on a post card will do nicely. Qantas, Union Square, Sam Francisco.

*Pronounce the Q as in Qantas.

QANTAS

AUSTRALIA'S OVERSEAS AIRLINE

Gossage's aim was, as ever, to involve his audience, and thousands of people duly joined in the fun. As you can see, he also sought to continue the conversation by inviting a further response at the end of the ad.

```
                    -4-

Oh hell, here is a radio commercial Freberg and I did once, oh
10 years age, but never produced, as I recall. I like it best:

First Man:      Hey, I got that jingle worked out for Pictsweet
                Frozen Foods.

Second man:     Good.

First Man:      Do you want to hear it?

Second man:     Sure

First man (sings): PICTSWEET, PICTSWEET, SOMETHING SOMETHING SOMETHING
                SOMETHING, SOMETHING

                PICTSWEET, PICTSWEET, SOMETHING, SOMETHING, SOMETHING
                SOMETHING, SOMETHING

                LAH DAH DAH DAH DAH DAH DAH DAH XXXXXX YOU AND ME

                LAH DAH DAH DAH DAH DAH DAH DAH QUALITY TOO

                PICTSWEET, PICSSWEET, WHERE THE MOUNTAINS MEET THE
                SEA

First man:      Well, how did you like it?

Second man:     Fine, but I'd tighten up those lyrics a little.
```

In the mid-'fifties Gossage and Stan Freberg brought a new style of anarchic humour to radio commercials. Here, in a letter to Barrows Mussey, Gossage reproduces his favourite radio script.

wing of the American advertising industry. He followed it up with an ad asking people to explain why there was no "u" in Qantas; 7,500 people wrote in. Then there was his collaboration with writer/actor Stan Freberg on behalf of Contadina Tomato Paste. What resulted was one of the first attempts at humerous radio commercials in the history of American advertising; and a promotion for Gossage. Just 12 months after starting as a junior copywriter, he was made vice-president.

For many that would have been an end in itself but titles never impressed Gossage and he quit because of the restrictions he felt he was working under. According to Alice Lowe who had followed his career ever since their first encounter at Joe Weiner's agency, "He worked briefly in several other San Francisco agencies but found the experience totally unsatisfactory." [18]

FIERD … FRIED … FEDIR … FDIER … FIRED

In his short career he'd already worked as a promotions manager, copywriter, art director and as a radio time buyer. His last assignment as a salaried employee was as an account executive at Guild, Bascom & Bonfigli. It ended unhappily for everyone except, that is, the people who mattered most in Gossage's eyes, the public.

The brief was to generate awareness of the Nucoa margarine brand name. While the standard response to such briefs involved a big TV and/or press budget, Gossage did something different. He ran a page advertisement in the *New Yorker* whose headline read, "New York's prayers go with Dudley!" and which went on to explain that Dudley was the light aircraft pilot who'd been tasked with signwriting the Nucoa brand name in the sky above Hollywood.

The media picked up on the story and each day reported that the word was misspelled differently: "NOOPS", "NEWCO", "NUCOV", "NOOCO"; with Dudley discussing his dilemma with his "coach", Gossage's collaborator, Stan Freberg. Finally, on Friday, he got NUCOA right.

The advertisement was a success, and engaged millions more people than would ever have noticed the standard TV campaign. And at a fraction of the cost, too. Unfortunately, one or two of those who did spot the campaign were senior Nucoa executives; and they were furious. Even today, in these supposedly ironic, irreverent times, few clients will countenance anyone messing with their brand name. In the conservative, cautious 'fifties such behaviour was anathema. They demanded heads, and Gossage was the first to the guillotine.

He must have climbed those steps with Sydney Carton's air of noble resignation. For as Alice Lowe concluded, "His insistence on trying out new ideas in spite of management's disapproval made him, in his own words, 'the most unemployable person I know'."[19] Given that recruitment profile, the only thing left was to go into business for himself. And that's what happened on 30 August, 1957 when, after months of soliciting from the man who'd originally turned him down, Gossage's name went above the door as a partner in the new agency Weiner & Gossage, Inc.

Chapter 2

A DIFFERENT TYPE
OF AGENCY

"IF SOMETHING'S WORTH DOING, IT'S WORTH OVERDOING"

When launching an agency, the partners usually look for a point of useful differ-ence that will make their business stand out from the crowd. By and large, this isn't based upon something new that hasn't been thought of before. It is informed more by the founders' experience of what was bad about the agencies in which they've previ-ously worked, and signals their intentions to avoid those shortcomings in their new venture.

So, for example, having worked in an agency that was unproductively top-heavy with client service, the ambitious new leaders might decide to dispense with that department completely. Or, having seen their old agency suffer because it was too hierarchical, the new one might boldly announce its intention to build success upon a totally flat structure.

Most new start-ups begin life as a vaguely contrarian conceit. Not Howard Luck Gossage's. He set out to create an agency that, in every aspect of its being, was unlike any of the major players in the American advertising industry.

First, the way they got paid.

Kicking against the "kick-backs"

Up until then agencies had made their money out of "the commission system". This was the 15% rebate they received when booking the space in which their advertis-ing would run. So if, for example, a newspaper charged $50,000 for a particular campaign to appear in its pages, then the agency received $7,500 just for placing the advertisements. Note that they weren't being paid for taking the client's brief, researching the market, working out the strategy, coming up with the creative idea, writing the copy or devising the layout. That was given away free. They derived all their money from the commission that was granted them by the media owners.

We'll get some idea of the size of that commission if we look at the kind of money being spent in the various media. In 1957, the year that Gossage founded his agency, $150 million was being spent on billboards and car cards; $300 million on radio commercials and programmes; $1 billion on television; $1.2 billion on newspaper advertisements; and $1.3 billion on advertisements in magazines.[1]

At 15%, even a small agency's "kick-back", as Gossage derisively called it, could easily be measured in six figure sums.

Gossage was appalled by a situation in which the agency that thrived best was the one which recommended ever higher expenditure on media. As he pointed out, a bad advertisement that ran twenty times earned twenty times more for the agency than a good one that ran once. To him this bred "a sort of immorality and mutual distrust similar to that which might prevail were the doctor paid for putting you in hospital rather than keeping you out of it – and was paid by the hospital at that."[2]

Joe Weiner and Howard Gossage broke ranks by insisting their clients buy less advertising not more. In fact, it was an article of faith with Gossage that if the advertisement was good enough then the audience would notice and you'd only need to run it once. As he said, "It's like sexual intercourse. You don't have to keep doing it nine months to have a baby. You do it right first time and after that it's tender loving care."[3]

Getting paid for ideas

This shift in emphasis from commission to creative meant Weiner & Gossage were paid for ideas. And paid royally, too. As Alice Lowe explains, "They employed a fee structure based on the value of the creative service which was higher than the standard 15% media commission granted to agencies. Their justification was that they offered only top-level talent to their clients and did not pass accounts along to lower echelons."[4]

As such, Weiner & Gossage was the first agency to live or die on the quality of its advertising. At the time there were two bigger agencies that were also renowned for their creative work, Ogilvy, Benson & Mather and Doyle Dane Bernbach, but neither had been bold enough to take that step. Indeed, it wasn't until 1960 that Ogilvy, Benson & Mather followed Weiner & Gossage's lead when they negotiated a fee for the work they were doing for Shell – and that move was made at the client's insistence.

Weiner & Gossage's decision to trade on their creative abilities caused quite a stir. As the advertising industry's paper, *Printers' Ink*, announced in a feature article on this radical new agency, "This is the story of two men whose sole merchandise is ideas."[5]

Back in 1957, this made Weiner & Gossage remarkable. They were also different because the emphasis on ideas meant they were what we nowadays call a "creative-led agency". According to Andrew Cracknell in his recent appraisal of the industry at mid-century, "In most agencies the creative work was merely a functional job. The power within the organisation rested with the account people .... Not even the creative director had much say .... It was the account men – almost exclusively men – who were the judge and executioner on all creative work, with the power to reject, edit and even personally rewrite if they so wished."[6]

The corollary of this was – and remains to this day – creative compromise. Account men second guessed the clients and gave them what they thought they would buy instead of what they knew they needed.

Apparently, there were no such shenanigans at Weiner & Gossage. Their positioning meant they were determined to *sell* the best work and make sure it ran – rather than pandering to the client or allowing them the final decision on how the advertising looked or what it said.*

As Jay Conrad Levinson, one of the first recruits to Weiner & Gossage, recalls: "Howard's clients' understanding of him was if he presented them an ad, they were not to change it. It was not an invitation to edit. And it was not a choice of ads. It was, 'This is the right thing for you right now. Let's do it'. And there was never any question about them altering the ads."[7]

The refusal to change things also applied to every word of body copy. This again put Gossage at odds with the way things worked in the Madison Avenue agencies. We get an impression of what it was like at, for example, McCann-Erickson from the painful memories of Bill Jayme. Direct mail specialist Jayme was the copywriter who came closest to Gossage's intimate style of conversational writing. He was so good that, after he left McCann-Erickson, he moved to San Fransisco, set up his own freelance business, and became the highest-paid copywriter in the world.

However, while at McCann-Erickson he lamented, "The copy went up to the copy chief, then through the copy vice-president, then the copy review board, then over to the client's assistant – some nitwit earning maybe 5 cents a week, and he made changes with his pencil – then to the client himself. Sometimes the only thing remaining that you had written, was the name of the product." [8]

It doesn't sound very enjoyable, does it?

---

*Nowadays it is commonplace to hear agencies chant the mantra: "Ideas ... ideas ... ideas". The only problem is that most contemporary agencies present exactly that: three ideas. And alongside the more innovative, and therefore challenging, work there are usually a couple of safer options which the client will tend to prefer because they make them feel more comfortable.

Having fun

Then again, as Jay Conrad Levinson recalls, enjoying things was another point of difference between Weiner & Gossage and its competitors, "What distinguished it was everybody was having fun, no one ever seemed under stress." The unconventional and easy-going atmosphere impressed the writer of an agency profile that appeared in the *Kansas City Star*, "Rule breaking could be forgiven. But what to many other admen is the most unprofessional cut of all, Gossage has great fun doing it . . . [what's more] the small staff seem pleased and happy with themselves, and go about their work at a leisurely pace."[9]

"Fun" and "leisurely" weren't words normally associated with advertising agencies at that time. Indeed, "advertising" was a synonym for "anxiety", and Madison Avenue was known as "Ulcer Gulch".[10] Here is Martin Mayer describing life there in his seminal work *Madison Avenue U.S.A.* (1958): "Many of the most important men in advertising work from their rising in the morning to their falling down at night. At the agencies, especially, the hours are long to the point of brutishness." In such a world "crisis is the normal state of affairs . . . [and] every night the briefcases and attaché cases go home stuffed with work . . . ."[11]

The impact on family life was devastating. In 1958, 1,100 advertising people were reminded briefly of their children when pollsters asked if they'd recommend the industry to their offspring. Only eight per cent said "yes".[12]

The relaxed ambiance also differentiated Gossage's agency in another way. Most of the great admen were distant, authority figures. Indeed, as is certainly the case today amongst the big names of US advertising, they demanded the kind of deference that, in comparison, would have made Louis XIV feel neglected.

We get an impression of this from Sally Kemp's recollections of Gossage's visits to his friend David Ogilvy's Madison Avenue office. "We would occasionally see David Ogilvy when we were in New York and I was very impressed with his office. One day a maid came in with a perfect grey silk uniform with a little apron and little white cap, and served beautiful tea with a silver service. We didn't do that at Howard's agency."[13]

Looking after the staff

No, there was no standing on ceremony there, for the boss was the most approachable of men. More than that, he took an active interest in his people. For example, decades before it became common practice in more enlightened businesses to develop what might be called a learning culture, he allowed staff members time off for extracurricular studies.

Alice Lowe explains, "I mentioned to Howard one day that I would like to be a docent [guide/lecturer] for the multi-billion dollar collection of Asian art which Avery Brundage was donating to the city, but required at least a half-day weekly for training for the next three years. He peered at me through horn-rimmed glasses to see if I was serious. When he saw that I was, he grinned and shook my hand. 'You shall be my contribution to culture', he announced grandly. He was pleased I wanted to expand my knowledge of Asian art and culture. With that, he left the office to buy me a book on Chinese art so I could start studying immediately. He gave me complete freedom of time so I could indulge whatever other interest I had at the museum."[14]

Gossage's involvement also extended to what we'd today call pastoral care. As Alice Lowe continues, "If you had something on your mind you could always go to him and ask him what he thought, and he would take it very seriously."[15]

Dugald Stermer the art director/designer who came to regard Gossage as a brother/father figure says, "I miss him every day .... . There has never been anyone to replace him in my life and there's never been anybody to whom I want to turn around and say 'did you hear what just happened?' or 'guess what I'm doing now' or 'do I take this on?'"[16]

You doubt whether that's the kind of relationship many young employees had with someone whose corner office overlooked 40th and Madison, yet it typified the *esprit de corps* that Gossage encouraged in his agency.

Dozens of roses and four-letter words

That's not to say that the love-in wasn't disturbed by a regular bust-up. Howard Gossage was not one to suffer fools gladly and, as his wife Sally explains, would express this with "salty" language before advising the person "there's the door. Now be sure it doesn't hit you on the ass on your way out."[17]

He held strong opinions, was often dismissive of those of others and, on occasion, was capable of causing offence. In fact, those occasions were pretty frequent. Alice Lowe recalls that whenever he'd upset someone, regardless of their sex, he'd send a dozen long-stemmed red roses. As she concedes, "We had a kind of staggering florists' bill".[18]

Gossage was definitely a man of his time. He drank, he smoked and he swore. And heavily in all three cases. As Alice Lowe continues, "Howard's command of profanity was as extensive as his knowledge of sentence structure, and as frequently used."[19]

He was certainly capable of doing and saying things that would offend today's guardians of political correctness. For instance, on one occasion he wrote to his friend, the writer Barrows Mussey, that his actress wife, Sally, who had a particularly large gay following, "had had more faggots at her feet than Joan of Arc." Ever the intellectual, he attributed this quote to the novelist Saul Bellow.[20]

The one-man team

When it came to working practices there was another aspect of Gossage's approach that was very much of its time.

Whereas Bill Bernbach at Doyle Dane Bernbach ultimately transformed the industry by his pairing together of his art directors and copywriters into idea-generating teams, Gossage stuck firmly to the old way. He, the copywriter, was responsible for having the creative idea which he then passed on to the art director who devised a complementary lay out.

As such, Gossage's style of headline writing was different to that of the Bernbach school i.e. the deft word play that interacted with the ad's visual to deliver the big creative idea. As we'll see, Gossage was more interested in writing a straighter, more direct headline that not only grabbed the reader's attention but was also news-worthy enough to generate headlines of its own.

Similarly, Gossage also dismissed the brainstorming techniques pioneered by Alex Osborn at Batten, Barton, Dustine & Osborn (and which today find expression in the craze for collaboration which insists that all good things come from collective effort). As he put it bluntly, "Most outstanding advertising comes from a creative dictatorship."[21] Sally Kemp is under no illusion about her husband's prowess as a team player: "He wasn't. He had a team but they were there to support him. He really was the voice. You couldn't see him sitting round a table saying 'what do you think of this?'"[22]

That's not to say that he didn't respect his colleagues. On the contrary. He knew he was working with some of the best professionals in the industry.

When Sally Kemp first met the people who worked with Gossage she was "struck by their graciousness. They were beautiful people. I don't know where he found them. I like to think they were born of his brow."[23] If that was the case then it was a brow unfurrowed by concerns about race, colour or creed.

Without prejudice

This again differentiated Gossage's agency from those established New York outfits where prejudice was common. Jerry Della Femina, who was to become one of the stars of the creative revolution in the 'sixties, explained in his memoirs that, "Advertising agencies in those days were broken down along ethnic lines. The Mad Men flourished in large Protestant agencies like J. Walter Thompson and N.W. Ayer, BBDO and Ted Bates."[24]

People like Della Femina, who were clearly of Italian or Jewish descent, were referred to as "ethnics" and advised to find work at "Seventh Avenue" agencies which usually had Jewish owners. This is what happened to the young Jerry Mander, who recalls an interview at a Park Avenue agency where he was told, "Your hair is a little kinky; you might want to try Seventh Avenue."[25]

Jerry Mander would be a late recruit to the Gossage agency. By then the hierarchy had established itself and, Gossage aside, his two most influential colleagues were both women. That, in itself, was unusual. But things were even more remarkable, for if Italians and Jews were unwelcome in many agencies then being Chinese was beyond the pale. And running the show for Gossage was Alice Lowe, a formidable lady of 100 per cent Chinese extraction.

Far from being embarrassed by Alice's origins, Gossage wanted her to, in her words, "Capitalize upon my Oriental background. He suggested that I use my Chinese name (which translated means 'Most Precious Jade')". Although Alice demurred, Gossage carried on addressing her by the respectful initials "M.P.J." or, more often, simply the affectionate nickname, "Presh."[26]

Bob & Howard & Marget & Alice

Such respect and affection were appropriate for, as Sally Kemp explains, "Alice Lowe really made everything around him work. She was probably the greatest gift that ever came into Howard's working life. Alice got everything going and made everything run exquisitely."[27] Alice herself is more practical in her description: "My role was that of the modern-day CEO which means in charge of everything: parties, running business, finance, hiring, firing, hitting deadlines, media buying ... everything you can think of. I did everything except for art direction and copy."[28]

If, in the early days, Gossage wrote all the copy then the art direction was done by two designers. Bob Freeman had the distinction of becoming a partner in the business in 1963 but it was the other designer, Marget Larsen, who was unquestionably in charge. Without a moment's hesitation, Jerry Mander described Larsen as "the world's greatest designer."[29] Dugald Stermer, who himself is acknowledged as being one of the finest designers of his generation, concurs. "Marget Larsen was the visual incarnation of Gossage's advertising. She gave it the look. It was stunning."[30]

Long after the Gossage agency was dissolved, a young Rich Silverstein, now of the successful advertising agency Goodby, Silverstein & Partners, made the pilgrimage to Marget Larsen's studio and, to this day, says her approval was the most meaningful compliment he's ever been paid.[31]

With her eye for design, understanding of balance and feeling for typography, Marget gave the new agency's advertising a unique appearance. But her influence didn't end there. For if the advertisements didn't look like those of any other agency, then neither did the offices. And, once again, this was Marget Larsen's doing.

The beautiful and enigmatic Marget Larsen relaxing at the Gossage family apartment. Rich Silverstein would eventually make a pilgrimage to her studio, and say that her approval was the most meaningful compliment he'd ever been paid.

The hippest agency in town ...

For the first three years, Weiner & Gossage was based at 149 California Street. As Jay Conrad Levinson has it, they were "nondescript offices with highly descript people."[32] It was Larsen's idea to set up shop in the louche Barbary Coast neighbourhood. As usual, Gossage deferred to her impeccable taste. Which meant that a decade before creative boutiques hit upon the idea of re-purposing old warehouses, factories, churches, schools and residential spaces, Gossage – or more accurately Marget Larsen – was transforming an old firehouse into an agency.

Here is how Alice Lowe described Larsen's creation: "As much of the original architectural feeling of the building was retained as possible .... Throughout the building, brick walls were left as they were except for a light coat of beige paint to blend them in with adjacent plain walls. Floors were all of gleaming random plank dark wood, some of it the original floorings; ceilings were covered with the same hammered gold leaf paper in square tile pattern used for the entrance halls; all the window ledges and display areas were finished with Italian marble in muted shades of orange."[33]

Visitors to the Firehouse conference room were invited to leave their graffiti on the wall. As we'll see in Chapter 5, one distinguished guest had his amended by an unimpressed critic.

Orange was Gossage's favourite colour. And, in the advertising agency that now occupies the building, the original bright orange carpet can still be seen in the tiny, ten square feet space at the top of the Firehouse which Gossage used as his bedroom while working flat out on his campaigns.

Unfortunately, there is now no evidence of the precious antiques that Larsen chose for the building: the 19th century, three-tier Dutch brass chandelier, the English walnut armchairs, the oriental rug with mellowed orange and blue geometric design. Thankfully, however, one piece remains with the Gossage family: the warped and worn 16th Century Spanish writing desk and cabinet which was hauled by slaves, set down in the field and used to write the orders of battle by Conquistador generals.

Compare all that with Martin Mayer's description of the decor at Young & Rubicam, one of Madison Avenue's biggest agencies: "A visitor to the executive floor of Y&R could be pardoned for feeling that he was in a bank: a long, spacious, deeply carpeted hall broken by a few counter-height partitions to establish areas for the widely spaced secretaries, doors opening into obvious (and almost identical) distinction, the monochrome green enforcing an impression of solidity."[34]

Not, as you might imagine, an environment wholly conducive to creative thinking.

... and the most happening

In contrast, Weiner & Gossage was less an agency and more a mix of social club and symposium. In fact, Gossage became known as "The Socrates of San Francisco" because of his penchant for leisurely talking around a subject for hours to fellow conversationalists who would drift in and out as the afternoon turned to evening.

The bar was always well-stocked and everyone was free to help themselves, with Gossage eagerly leading by example with a large Paddy Irish whiskey and soda. Very often these long conversations had nothing to do with the clients' business; people were invited to drop in and just spend the day in animated discussion with the agency boss.

If we recall Gossage's childhood and remember his craving for attention, then here in the Firehouse was the audience and the company he'd always been seeking. As Jerry Mander says, "Howard was a fantastically entertaining, very, very funny man. He really liked to be around creative people, of any kind, or intellectuals. He was hungry for [that]. He loved being around smart, intelligent, funny, creative people of any discipline. There were a lot of political people, a lot of artists .... What he lived for was the exchange of ideas and the exchange of experience, and I think that was his greatest craving."[35]

Tom Wolfe thought that Gossage's laugh was "a cosmic laugh because whenever I heard it, it propelled your mind beyond what you were hearing in that instant and whatever had taken place in that instant, on to something that went far beyond."

Looking back on those gatherings, Sally Kemp suggests that, "He managed to take the 18th Century Salon and put it slap bang into the middle of the 20th Century."[36] If that was the case then there was nothing of the silk-hatted dilettante in Gossage's make-up. Far from it. A fan of jests and japes, he loved to laugh and, according to friend and journalist Tom Wolfe, that laugh was something to behold. "I always thought of [it] as a cosmic laugh because whenever I heard it, it propelled your mind beyond what you were hearing in that instant and whatever had taken place in that instant, on to something that went far beyond.... He was born with the gift of laughter and a sense that the world was mad."[37]

Magicking up the Mariachis

It wasn't, however, just the boss's laughter that drowned out the sound of heated debate and learned discourse. Very often it was raucous racket of Senor Salvador Padilla's eight-piece Mariachi Band.

Mariachi music was a feature of the famous Firehouse lunches which Alice Lowe organised with a mix of military precision and a magician's sleight of hand. Applying what she called the "Instant Party Plan" she could, within minutes, transform a working office into a bar, buffet restaurant and dance floor.[38]

Often such parties were celebrating a visit by one of Gossage's friends. And what friends they were: John Steinbeck, John Huston, Terry Thomas, Jessica Mitford, Doctor Benjamin Spock. As well as the great and the good, there were also the up-

and-coming. A young Joan Rivers was once seen standing nervously on the sidelines; on another occasion the model and rising Hollywood star, Candice Bergen, was in attendance.

As Sally Kemp recalls in relation to the Steinbecks and the Spocks, "Every time one of these wonderful people would show up … would be an excuse for a party and Howard would call everyone and there would be food and everyone would be taken care of and made to feel welcome. It was such a wide range of people: news-papermen … theologians … actors. They'd come for lunch, stay for cocktails and dance all night."[39]

And in the thick of it all would be the host, delighting in the high-brow, high jinks; encouraging ever more exuberant excesses with one of his favourite sayings, "If something's worth doing, it's worth overdoing."[40]

Pressures of work

If, however, Gossage was always eager to overdo the fun at Weiner & Gossage then his immersion in the work was just as exaggerated.

Given Gossage's inability to work in a team, and the agency's promise never to palm clients off with secondary talent, it was he who was responsible for all the creative ideas. This put him under tremendous pressure. Sally Kemp was witness to this: "At times he was literally in despair and I can remember him tearing his hair and saying 'I feel like I'm digging in my skull for gold and my skull is going to be empty and I'm going to have nothing but gold fillings under my nails and there's going to be this empty skull.'"[41]

His *modus operandi* was to retire to his office for days on end, emerging occasionally to request hot chocolate or some other stimulant. After a week or so, he would reappear with the one advertisement he was going to present to the client. It would comprise the headline and usually a sub-headline plus every one of what might stretch to over 1,000 words of body copy.

Actually that body copy was always subject to amendment. For, like most great copywriters, Gossage was never satisfied, and would re-write up to the last minute of the deadline. In fact, he was such a perfectionist that his colleagues joked that one day he'd insist on amending his copy *after* the ad had appeared in the newspaper.

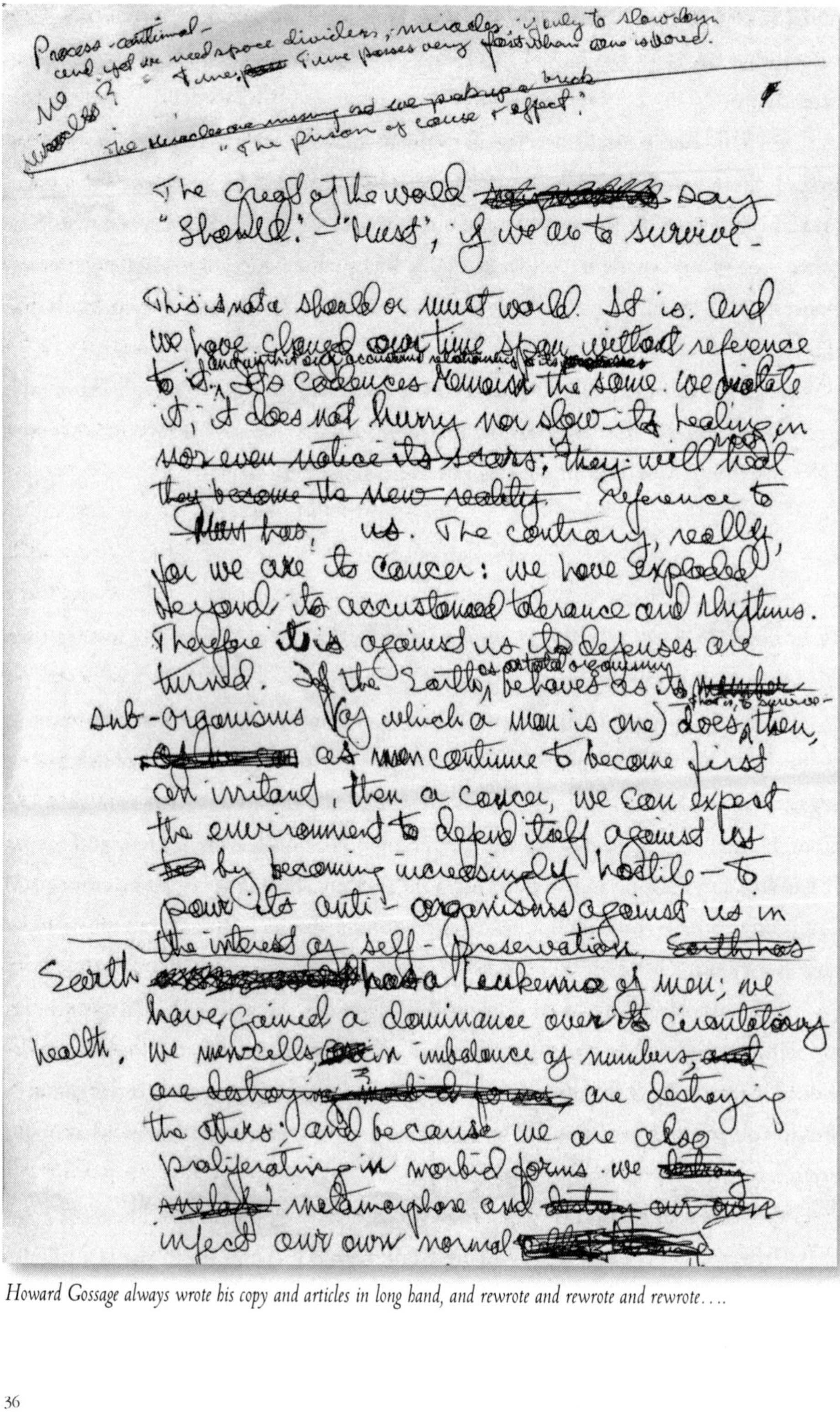

[Handwritten manuscript — partially legible]

Process continual —
and if we need space dividers, miracles, a way to slow down
NO? = Time, time passes very fast than one is bored.
The miracles one missing and we pick up a brick
"The prison of cause & effect."

The great of the world ~~say~~ say
"should": 'must', if we are to survive.

This is not a should or must world. It is. And
we have cleared our time span without reference
to it, its cadences remain the same. We violate
it; it does not hurry nor slow its healing in
nor even notice its scars; they will heal
they become its new reality. Reference to
us. The contrary, really,
for we are its cancer: we have exploded
beyond its accustomed tolerance and rhythms.
Therefore against us its defenses are
turned. If the Earth behaves as its organism
sub-organisms (of which a man is one) does, then,
as men continue to become first
an irritant, then a cancer, we can expect
the environment to defend itself against us
by becoming increasingly hostile — to
pour its anti-organisms against us in
the interest of self-preservation. Earth has
Earth has a leukemia of men; we
health, we men cells, in imbalance of numbers, and
are destroying are destroying
the others; and because we are also
proliferating in morbid forms we
metamorphose and infect our own normal

Howard Gossage always wrote his copy and articles in long hand, and rewrote and rewrote and rewrote….

This need to rewrite was an old trait. *San Francisco Chronicle* columnist and friend Herb Caen recalled a secretary at Gossage's first agency, Brisacher, Wheeler & Staff lamenting, "Just because he dictates a letter and I type it doesn't mean it will ever reach the person to whom he's addressed it. He writes, revises, revises. revises and then decides not to send it." When asked why she put up with him she said, "It was all very much worth it. He's magnificent".[42]

Gossage was also demanding of himself and others when it came to the usage of the English language. As Dugald Stermer recalls, "He was very particular about grammar and syntax. I once made the mistake of describing something as "a fun event". He looked at me and said 'Dugald, *fun* is not an adjective'."[43]

Black moods would descend when ideas wouldn't come. Gossage would often stay away from work, discard his immaculate suit, shirt and tie, and mooch around in an old sweater and slacks.

Even allowing himself such an error, Gossage would never have used "fun" to describe his view of work. While he was elated when campaigns proved successful, his joy disappeared when the next assignment arrived and he realised he had to deliver yet again.

When the big idea proved elusive he became morose and uncommunicative, and even took to his bed. If he did speak it was usually at the top of his voice. These black moods took their toll on everyone, and Gossage realised that he needed the freedom to resign a piece of business when the creative process became too painful.

Quitting an account ...

Again this differentiated Weiner & Gossage from the rest of the field, for few agencies have ever adopted such a stance. In fact, the general rule is to hang on to the client's business until your account director is carried bodily from the client's premises. Especially if that account is the agency's biggest earner.

But at the Firehouse, such financial considerations didn't appear to bother Howard Gossage. Paul Masson Wines was the agency's largest account and Gossage had created some excellent work for them. However, after several years, he felt he'd grown too stale to deliver to the same standard. This he couldn't countenance. So he came up with what he hoped was a solution.

According to Dugald Stermer, "He said, 'why don't you come and consult at the agency?' He wanted me to come in once a week for four or five hours. 'Your basic job is to tell me why I should continue with Paul Masson Wines.' So I would do sketches, I would come up with ideas for campaigns, crazy stuff hoping that Gossage would take an interest. And I did it off and on for about six months and then I said, 'Gossage, I've come up with nothing that you're interested in' and he said, 'OK, well I'd better resign the account then ... if I'm not interested, nobody else will be.' And he went to see the president of Paul Masson."

Apparently the conversation went like this:

Howard Gossage: "I've got to quit this account because I can't stand your advertising."

President of Paul Masson Wines: "But you do the advertising."

Howard Gossage: "I know, that's why I'm quitting the account." [44]

... and spinning a story

It's a wonderful anecdote, and one which is often repeated by those who revere the Gossage memory. However, at this point it might be worth a few words of caution in case we transform this most human of individuals into a plaster saint.

As we'll see, Gossage was a master of PR for his clients, and we should bear that in mind when reading his version of events regarding himself and his agency.

For he was certainly capable of applying an element of spin in order to promote the images of both.

For example, Gossage was not alone in thinking his ads were dull. As a *Business Week* profile concluded, his "ads for Paul Masson Vineyards are unexceptional and not terribly exceptional."[45] Moreover, what is never mentioned about that famous conversation with the president of Paul Masson Wines is that the client was unhappy. As Gossage explained in a letter to his friend Barrows Mussey, "They want hand-holding and 'marketing', whatever that may be".

Gossage's agency simply wasn't designed to offer the kind of client service that other agencies provided. So, it seems he got his resignation in first and then devised a very shrewd exit strategy. "As it happens, they did as I advised and went to Doyle Dane Bernbach, but only after I had agreed to keep them as consulting clients and for design and other things; i.e. all but marketing and advertising. It works out very well for us, just about as much money as before and without all that incomprehensibility."[46]

The above details notwithstanding, stories like "I can't stand your advertising" have become the stuff of legend. As Jeff Goodby, the co-founder of Goodby, Silverstein & Partners says, "I don't remember ever reading or hearing a story where he took a financial aspect of something into consideration. Ever. You've got to love that."[47]

Yes, you do. But not, one supposes, if you'd been called Joe Weiner who, not unnaturally for a partner in the business, was more interested in getting new clients through the door than waving business goodbye.

Parting with Joe Weiner – and client service

Given the differing attitudes, a split was inevitable and it came in April, 1963.

The primary reason lay in Gossage's feeling that his partner was putting him under too much pressure by chasing too much business. As far as Gossage was concerned, it was easy to win new clients but it was a hell of a lot harder to keep them happy by doing the kind of work for which the agency was famous.

Gossage was unwilling to compromise on the quality of his output and, in order to maintain standards, was determined to limit the demands that were made on his time.

Weiner, a natural salesman, couldn't accept this, so he had to go. His terms were, however, exacting for he demanded an exorbitant amount of money plus ownership of the Firehouse in which the agency was based.

Alice Lowe remembers being appalled at these financial demands and urged Gossage to resist. To no avail. Gossage didn't care how much it cost, just as long as he was free of his partner and in complete control of the agency.

Although Weiner's name was replaced by that of art director, Bob Freeman, to become Freeman & Gossage, the agency philosophy remained the same. If anything it became more radical. That's because Gossage never replaced Weiner with a senior client-facing account executive. Which meant that forty years before other creative agencies were to experiment without a client service department, Gossage was putting that plan into action – with himself as the main client contact.

To make this work, he made it a rule only to deal with the president of the client business. Again, this was caused by his contempt for teamwork, committees and the lesser mortals who participated in both. As he explained, "The top man is likely to be more creative than subordinates he has hired to follow him around with butterfly nets. He can convey more to another creative person than he can to either his advertising manager or account executive. This sort of contact eliminates much of the vitiation an idea inevitably undergoes in its progress through echelons and committees."[48]

It also put even more pressure on the boss of the agency who now had to be head of client service, managing director and creative director rolled into one. We'll see that within a few years this became too much for Gossage. But, immediately post-Joe Weiner, it allowed him the control he needed to do things the way he wanted – and the biggest thing he wanted was to stay small.

Small is beautiful

Size had become a fixation with Gossage and he revelled in the paradox of achieving national fame yet remaining what he called a "Mickey Mouse agency".[49]

As Dugald Stermer recalls, "A writer from *Fortune* magazine was commissioned to go out to San Francisco and feature this hot advertising guy and do a profile of the agency. So he came out and had an appointment with Howard and finally arrived at the Firehouse and looked around and there were about three people in the office including Howard. And the journalist said 'This can't be the Freeman & Gossage agency I've heard of.' Howard says, 'Yeah.' And he said, 'Well, it's awfully small.' and Howard laughs, 'Small? We're not even the largest agency on the block!'"[50]

The aim was never to grow beyond 15 people. To this day that remains the antithesis of pretty much every business plan any agency has ever written itself. And it was particularly perverse at a time when the industry was pumping millions of dollars into a mergers and acquisitions bubble. No-one doubted that growth was the only strategy. As Roy S. Durstine of Batten, Barton, Durstine & Osborn, who had billings in excess of $200 million, said "No agency is small by choice."[51]

No, throughout the industry, the overriding goal was constant growth, regardless of the pressure this put upon staff and existing client relationships. Senior executives were perpetually on the lookout for newer, bigger-spending accounts and would happily resign a long-standing client if a more lucrative competitor of that client became available.

Gossage, on the other hand, was quite happy to turn work away. Sally Kemp tells the story of one potential client's visit to the agency: "Volkswagen came to him a couple of years before they were going to introduce the 'Bug' into this country and they wanted him to do the advertising, which would have been an extraordinary coup. So he looked at the car and then told them 'You know, this product is like a Hershey Bar'. Hershey Bars had never done any advertising, they hadn't had to. He said, 'You don't need to advertise this. It isn't necessary. It's going to sell itself.' So they went somewhere else and somebody else made millions."[52]

Sally's "somebody else" was Doyle Dane Bernbach, and the resulting campaign brought the agency more than just "millions". The brilliant VW work catapulted the creative hotshop to national prominence. As Stephen Fox says in *The Mirror Makers* (1997), "For years it exercised incalculable power over the collective creative unconsciousness of the business."[53]

Had he not been so frank, such recognition could have been Gossage's, and the boost from the VW business could have put his agency in the big league. But, unlike other agency heads, Gossage did not want to be big and he refused to chase business. Indeed, he made a habit of giving it away and, as we've already seen with Paul Masson Wines, Doyle Dane Bernbach was Gossage's agency of choice when it came to recommending someone to take on the business he had decided to either forego or decline.

Death of a president

It was DDB's creative leader Bill Bernbach who coined the phrase, "It isn't a principle until it costs you money."[54] This was a noble sentiment that Gossage, one feels, would have endorsed.

Take, for example, what happened in the aftermath of the assassination of President John F. Kennedy on November 22, 1963.

Kennedy was shot in Dallas, the HQ of one of Gossage's largest accounts, the American Petrofina Company (Fina). Gossage's point of contact at Fina, Jack Shea Jr., felt that his fellow citizens were implicated in the crime – and was determined to do something about it.

Gossage was a huge fan of Kennedy and, according to his wife Sally, wept for days after his death. However, as Sally recalls, the mourning suddenly ended with a dash to Dallas and several days spent locked in a hotel room with Jack Shea and a steady stream of journalists.

The result of this activity appeared in the 24 March, 1964 edition of *Look* magazine. *Memo from a Dallas Citizen* by Shea, with Gossage's ghost-writing help, castigated Dallas's civic leaders for allowing an atmosphere of bigotry and prejudice to fester in the city prior to and after the assassination. Shea's fellow citizens were not happy and neither were his employers who demanded that

Shea sign an agreement that, in future, all public statements be approved by the company.

Shea, by nature a cautious man who avoided controversy, stuck courageously to his guns and quit. Gossage, by nature a reckless man who loved a commotion, was with him at New York's Lombardy Hotel when he made the decision. Without hesitation, he called Peter Bart, the advertising columnist at the *New York Times* and announced that his agency was resigning the business.

While Gossage soon got over the loss of Fina, he was changed forever by the death of JFK. As we'll see in Chapter 7, the impact took a couple more years to work itself out into action. But when it did, its effect was dramatic.

Meanwhile, the need to make good the loss of Fina's revenue didn't change Gossage's approach to business. As Alice Lowe explained, "He had numerous opportunities to merge, handle larger accounts, or become an independent advertising consultant for various concerns at $50,000 or $100,000 each, any combination of which would have assured him a generous financial return. But they would have also required sacrificing his hard-won independence, and that he was unwilling to give up for any amount of money."[55]

He could certainly have shipped out east and worked on Madison Avenue. He was friendly with David Ogilvy and occasionally showed him his advertisements before they ran. He even paid Ogilvy the compliment of parodying one of his finest ads. Whereas Ogilvy had written: "At 60 miles an hour the loudest noise in the new Rolls-Royce comes from the electric clock", Gossage had run an advertisement for his client Land-Rover that replaced the last two words with "roar of the engine". Ogilvy was impressed and it would have been easy for Gossage to sell out to him, or other of his rivals, and take a top executive's role amongst the Mad Men.

He always refused, however, and his clinging to the freedom to work his way bordered on the obsessive. But what drove it?

Staying independent

As we'll see in Chapters 7 and 8, he had a deep-seated philosophical aversion to "bigness" of any kind – be it governmental or business. To him its baleful effects were all too evident in every aspect of modern existence.

We'll explore this later but if, as we'll see, he knew what was wrong with the world then he must also have known what was amiss with Howard Gossage.

Clearly he was too headstrong and, some would say, arrogant to work with a team. Indeed, it was the realisation that he was unmanageable that had prompted him to start his own agency in the first place. And then it was his need for complete control that caused him to oust his partner, regardless of the cost.

Even the presence of another copywriter was intolerable. As he said in one speech, "My own ego is so strong that I can scarcely bear to have another copywriter around at all."[56]

What's more, he was unwilling and probably unable to work on the mass-market brands that provided the vast majority of the big agencies' revenue. In fact, he would only take on a piece of business whose target audience's tastes and preoccupations mirrored his own. As Sally Kemp recalls he would say, "I write about what interests me and only that. I assume there are others who share my interests."[57]

Such self-indulgence would never have been tolerated in another agency. Nor would his single-minded focus on one media. This was the era of television and it was in TV that creatives made their name, and agencies made their money. Yet Gossage never attempted a big TV campaign. He was content to specialise in press advertising. More specifically, whenever possible, he would only work on advertisements that appeared in *The New Yorker* magazine.

This, by definition, made him a niche player whose agency was not what we'd nowadays call scalable. And Gossage must have known that.

But there's another reason why Gossage didn't want to lose his independence: the overriding fear of falling into the category of advertising that he despised: the thoughtless, expensive, repetitive, hard sell that characterised most of the creative work that came out of Madison Avenue in the 1950s and early '60s.

Indeed, it was his deep-seated contempt for such work that led Gossage to not only start a different type of agency but, most importantly, to reject the techniques and style of his contemporaries and create a totally new kind of advertising.

Chapter 3

A NEW KIND
OF ADVERTISING

"PEOPLE READ WHAT
INTERESTS THEM,
AND SOMETIMES
IT'S AN AD"

If Howard Gossage disliked the advertising his peers were producing then he wasn't alone. Everyone knew that the industry in the 1950s was undergoing one of its creative low points.

Only the work by those up-and-coming creative-led agencies to which we've already referred – Ogilvy, Benson & Mather and Doyle Dane Bernbach – shone consistently. As a result they attracted a hugely disproportionate share of the trade papers' attention. As the unashamed self-publicist David Ogilvy pointed out, "We're only the fiftieth largest or something like that. But have you noticed that we're the most talked-about agency in town?"[1]

Quite simply, that was because the work of the bigger, more established organisations wasn't worth talking about. As Stephen Fox sums up in *The Mirror Makers*, it was "safe and dull, without flair or distinction. The memorable ads seemed especially good because there was so little competition .... All through the 1950s, advertising people deplored the lack of creativity among both practitioners and products."[2]

No one deplored that lack of creativity more than Howard Gossage.

As Professor Greg Pabst, Program Director, Advertising, at the University of San Francisco explains, "Howard Gossage hated the cliché admen who were on Madison Avenue using their scientific methods to bang, bang, bang their message into people's heads .... I think he hated that whole school. It was so easy in the 'fifties to do a roadblock on a Sunday night when everyone was watching one of three channels. All they had to do was buy a spot on each channel so the viewer couldn't avoid seeing it .... It cost lots of money but too many people in the 'fifties thought that a big budget was a big idea."[3]

Rosser Reeves and his USP

Pabst is right about Gossage's feelings. He made no secret of his contempt for what was then the dominant school of advertising – and its ultra-strict dean of studies, Rosser Reeves.

Actually, you can't help thinking that Gossage and Reeves, who was the head of the huge Ted Bates agency, would have got on well had they worked in different lines of business. Like Gossage, Reeves was a colourful, charismatic character.

Indeed, when that creative star of the 'sixties and 'seventies, Ed McCabe, finally encountered Reeves he described him as the only adman he ever met "who most closely defined the word 'cool'." This must have baffled McCabe, because Reeves was anathema to most creative types. Indeed, as McCabe said, "In advertising he was the archetypal bad guy".[4]

What provoked such a response was Reeves's unwavering faith in what he called The Unique Selling Proposition (USP). He explained the three tenets of this theory in his book *Reality in Advertising* (1961):

1) "Each advertisement must make a proposition to the consumer ... each advertisement must say to each reader: 'Buy this product, and you will get this specific benefit'."

2) "The Proposition must be one that the competition either cannot, or does not, offer."

3) "The Proposition must be so strong that it can move the mass millions, i.e., pull over new customers to your product."[5]

Once formulated, Reeves insisted that the Unique Selling Proposition remain the sole focus of all the advertising that was executed for that client. In itself, this was a sound strategy. People are primarily interested in the benefit a product brings them, so alerting prospects to that benefit makes good business sense.

It was, however, Reeves's approach to the "alerting" bit that caused creatives like McCabe and Howard Gossage to demonise him. For once the USP had been found, Reeves reckoned "the rest is just wordsmithing"[6]. As he said, "I never tried to make *interesting* commercials .... any good copywriter can write a good ad."[7]

According to Reeves, all the copywriter had to do was come up with a catchy phrase or jingle, and then rely on a media spend sufficient to imprint that mnemonic on to the mind of the American people.

A privilege, not a right

It was here that Reeves parted company with Gossage and the other creative-led agencies of the day. Foremost amongst those agencies was Doyle Dane Bernbach, which regarded the nailing of the proposition as just the halfway stage in the creative process. Thereafter,

DDB's teams strove for a big creative idea that would bring that proposition to life by dramatising or demonstrating it in a way that was not intrusive but actually interesting, imaginative and original.

David Ogilvy had his own creative approach but was essentially in the same camp. As he wrote in the mid-'fifties, "Unless your advertising contains a big idea, it will pass like a ship in the night."[8] We don't know Reeves's retort to his brother-in-law Ogilvy, but he would probably have said: "Unless, of course, you sail your ship past the customer at 15 minute intervals throughout the night blasting the same jingle at full volume."

In an interview with *Advertising Age* in 1965 Reeves explained that his method "may often entail the use of techniques that the copywriter might describe as terribly dull."[9] In the same article he revealed that one client had been happy to spend $86,400,000 on one advertisement in order to get what some of his peers might regard as his "terribly dull" message across.[10] Here, writ large, were the ills of the commission system's payment model that Gossage so despised. For it's easy to work out Ted Bates's 15% commission on that kind of media spend.

Gossage wasn't to be intimidated by the industry's most influential agency head and condemned the style and content of the advertising that Reeves championed. On one occasion he continued his critique over dinner with Reeves himself.

As he explained in a letter to his friend Barrows Mussey, "All went more or less smoothly until Rosser, who could bear it no longer, said: 'Tell me, Howard, why some people didn't like my book?'.... I said, 'Well, you are an intelligent man, and, I'm sure, a responsible one. It seemed to me that somewhere in there you should have had a chapter, a paragraph, a sentence, that indicated a proper respect for the opinion of mankind.'

"There was much more. But the high point, perhaps, was when were were talking about the most disliked commercial I could think of. I said it was Dristan's draining sinuses .... 'O.K.', he said 'don't you think the manufacturer of that product has a right to make a living?' I said, 'That he didn't have a right to do anything on my time, that advertising wasn't a right, it was a privilege.' He said, 'All right, there are 9,000,000 people in this country suffering from sinus trouble. Don't you think they are entitled to relief?' I said, 'Rosser, there are 195,000,000 people in this country who take a shit every day. I just don't want them to do it in my living room.'"[11]

-2-

was an exact parody of one of Ogilvy's ads. I got his permission to
do it. Ixxxx The Headline was "At 60 miles an hour the loudest noise
in the new Land-Rover is the roar of the engine". I copied everything
except writing style and content (feeling my own had merit). Well it
was splendid and sold cars like crazy. I gave a copy to David at
dinner the night it came out and he was so delighted, as well he should
have been, that he insisted on reading it aloud to me.* I forget what
the point to this story is. Oh, yes, one time earlier I ran an ad for a
snuff company (which we own) and I showed it to David and pointed out that
it followed his notion that the coupon should be at the top. He said,
"Oh, I'm sorry, I have evidence that would suggest that this isn't true"
(his rule that it would pull better; it didn't).

Bernbach I have found a very didactic sort of man firmly convinced that
his way is the only way. One time I was chatting with him about ads,
~~XXXXXXXXXXXXXXXXXXXXXXXXXXXXXXXXXXXXX~~ I believe he was vaguely
aware that I was in advertising, and I said, in answer to his statement
that thorough knowledge of a client's processes was absolutely essential,
that I had never visited a client's plant ever. (Rule: Never visit
the factory). He was outraged. He has the calm assurance of a Christian
Scinee practitioner so he managed to hold it in.

Would you like to hear about my lunch with Rosser Reeves? Lovely. Do
you know John Metcalf of Hobson Bates? Well John was there, too. All
went more or less smoothly until Rosser, who could bear it no longer,
said: ~~Iffekkpxxxxi~~ "Tell me, Howard, why some people didn't like my book".
I made little distressed moues because just the week before I had been
quoted in Advertising Age as saying I wouldn't watch TV even if Ix it
was Rosser Reeves and Frank Stanton playing ~~xxxxx~~ catch with a porcupine
because afterwards I'd have to watch the victor deliver a Gillette
commercial from the locker room. "No, no, nothing personal, but tell
me why some people didn't like a book that was assuredly sound."

I said, "Well, you are an intelligent man, and,I'm sure, a responsible
one. It seemed to me that somewhere in there you should have had a
chapter, a paragraph, a sentence, that indicated a proper respect for
the opinion of mankind".

There was much, much more. But the high point, perhaps, was when we
were talking about the ~~xxxxixxxxxxxxxxxixxxixxxxxkxxxthxixxxxixxxxtxxtxxxxxx~~
~~dxxxppxxxx~~ most disliked commercial I could think of. I said it was
Dristan's draining ~~xxx~~ sinuses, I guessed. (He thought I was going to
say Anacin, but I was adamant). "O.K., he said, "don't you think the
manufacturer of that product has a right to make a living?" I said that
he didn't have a right to do anything on my time, that advertising wasn't
a right it was a privilege. He said, "All right, there are 9,000,000
people in this country suffering from sinus trouble. Don't you think
they are entitled to ~~xxxxxxx~~ relief?" I said, "Rosser, there are
195,000,000 people in this country who take a shit every day, I just
don't want them to do it in my living room".

*I inscribed it: "To David; Imitation is the sincerest form of larceny".

Gossage had very different relationships with the three giants of the advertising industry. Here in a letter to Barrows Mussey dated 3 September, 1965 he describes his encounters with David Ogilvy, Bill Bernbach and Rosser Reeves.

What's the point of advertising?

It was an argument that always earned Gossage an audience and, ever eager for the spotlight to be on himself and his agency, one he frequently made from the speaker's podium and in the pages of the trade press.

Typical was the occasion on which he was asked if advertising was worthwhile and concluded, "From an economic point of view, I don't think that most of it is. From an aesthetic point of view I'm damn sure it's not; it is thoughtless, boring and there is simply too much of it."[12]

As regards the "too much of it", Gossage had concluded that most advertising could be dispensed with, save for that which performed one of two vital functions.

The first was the provision of newsworthy information about products or services; for example, a genuinely useful new version of an existing product or the launch of an innovative new service. Similarly, Gossage also saw classified and job advertisements as useful information, and felt that food and fashion ads in magazines were also a good idea. Either way, the arbiter would always be the editor of the magazine. In Gossage's view, it was they and they alone (not the advertiser) who understood that magazine as a totality – editorial and advertising – and it was they (not the advertiser) who had the reader's interest at heart.

There was only so much real news to report so the first category would, by definition, be pretty small. In which case, the rest of advertising would, as normal, be concerned with the promotion of existing products and services.

According to Gossage, however, the only type that should be allowed was that which was as entertaining and interesting as the editorial that surrounded it. Again, if the advertising wasn't up to the feature-writing standard of the magazine then the editor had every right to reject it.

Clearly, if Rosser Reeves and his aversion to making "interesting commercials" represented the prevailing mood, then very few advertisements on air or in the 'papers would have passed Gossage's editorial test.

Saying something interesting

It must be said that, while it guaranteed media attention, it took courage to criticise the contemporary creative scene. As Larry Dobrow explains in his excellent survey of the period *When Advertising Tried Harder*, the competitors Gossage disparaged "were not tired or weak or inefficient agencies ready to pass from the scene. McCann-Erickson, J. Walter Thompson, Batten, Barton, Durstine & Osborn and Young & Rubicam … were growing, aggressive, powerful and intelligent companies themselves. They had impeccable credentials, excellent reputations. loyal clients, talented personnel and clout!"[13]

And they were no doubt willing to use that clout with the trade press and trade bodies to disparage some upstart from a tiny agency on the far distant west coast. Rosser Reeves could certainly defend himself against what he called the "artsy-craftsy crowd." In what could be construed as a thinly-veiled attack on Gossage he told an editor at *Advertising Age*, "Some of the greatest copywriters, some of the legendary copywriters in the business are legendary only because they haven't been caught out."[14]

Gossage was fortunate in having a couple of acknowledged greats alongside him. Bill Bernbach's occasional critiques carried most weight, but generally he was more concerned with maintaining the high standards of his own creative department than improving those of the industry. As he explained, "I make ads, not speeches."[15]

David Ogilvy showed no such reticence. "The Showman" is how Bernbach dismissively (in private) referred to the British ex-pat who, like Howard Gossage, never missed the opportunity to speak out and grab a headline.[16] In response to Reeves's rejection of "interesting commercials" Ogilvy announced, "You cannot bore people into buying your product; you can only *interest* them in buying it."[17] This echoed Gossage's own adage, "People read what *interests* them, and sometimes it's an ad".[18]

If, as it seems, the two men were agreed on the importance of saying something interesting, they each had a very different approach to achieving it. Then again, that's not surprising given the opposite directions they took in search of a better style of advertising.

Finding a better way

First, Ogilvy. Like Gossage, he began his copywriting career late in life. But Ogilvy, who started aged 39, made up for lost time by immersing himself in books by, and about, the industry's leaders. He was in thrall to such luminaries as Albert Lasker, Raymond Rubicam, Claude Hopkins, Leo Burnett and, in a strange on/off relationship, his brother-in-law Rosser Reeves. Ogilvy made no secret of his debt to these men, and explained his own success by appropriating Sir Isaac Newton's quotation, "If I have seen further than others, it is because I have stood on the shoulders of giants."

Gossage, on the other hand, had no interest in the legend and lore of the business. In all his writings and speeches, there is no reference to Ogilvy's heroes.

Nor, despite his respect for both Ogilvy and Bernbach, did he seem too interested in his contemporaries. In 1963, the president of the trade paper *Printers' Ink* asked Gossage if he'd join a handful of other leading figures in contributing to the paper's 75th anniversary issue. The request was for Gossage's views on the industry in general and its leading copywriters in particular.

Gossage's handwritten response read, "Sorry to fail you but I simply don't have the time before the first of the month to tackle the assignment. I'm looking over parts 1 and 3 and find I know remarkably little about copywriters save myself. I've always been a loner."[19]

On a later occasion, *Printers' Ink* asked Gossage to contribute to a feature called "The ad I'll never forget". The ad he chose was certainly a classic of its kind. But it wasn't the kind *Printers' Ink* was expecting. As he explained in a letter to his friend Barrows Mussey, it was "a full page for a haberdasher in the Connellsville, Pa. paper around 1925. Huge wood-type headline: MONSTER SHIRT SALE. Unfortunately an R got left out."[20]

Ideas beyond advertising

While this is a classic example of Gossage's irreverence, it also shows that, unlike most people in the industry, Gossage wasn't interested in the internal and eternal debate about what was the best ad and who was the hottest writer. The "loner" was consciously trying to remain an outsider because, as we'll see, he felt that was the only way he could discover a more intelligent, responsible way of using advertising as a communications medium.

As Alice Lowe recalls, "Gossage's restless mind was in a continual ferment about advertising. He studied it with tireless energy – not to find fault, but to try to understand how it came to be what it is and how it might be changed. To this end, he exchanged voluminous correspondence with people in the field as well as thoughtful observers outside of advertising."[21]

The people "in the field" were some help but Gossage despaired of their general lack of curiosity. As he told students at Pennsylvania State University where he delivered a series of lectures in 1963, "There is precious little awareness, and no real enquiry into the economic, sociologic or philosophic bases of advertising."[22]

As to books about writing advertising, he was equally dismissive: "I can't think of any good books on how to make ads. Most of them are the unreadable in full pursuit of the unteachable."[23]

Disillusioned by his industry peers, he became convinced that it was impossible for anyone to recognise the true nature of their situation whilst they were immersed in that milieu. As he said, "We don't know who it was discovered water, but we're pretty sure it wasn't a fish". In fact, he maintained that the best advertising "will come from men from outside the prevailing environment. They will either come from another culture, another country, or be men who got into the business late in life after doing much else. ... Often they will be a combination of some or all these things. At any rate, they will do things which seem normal to them, but that seem extraordinarily perceptive to us."*[24]

Instead of studying advertising, Gossage looked to those "outside the prevailing environment" and steeped himself in more esoteric, demanding disciplines. Alice Lowe continues, "He possessed insatiable intellectual curiosity and was an omnivorous reader. Whenever he came across a writer with an unusual idea, or one who

---

*In 1964, this extra-environmental theory led Gossage to set up a consultancy with surgeon, psychiatrist and ventriloquist Dr. Gerald Feigen. They reckoned that most agencies foisted their specialism upon a client regardless of whether that was the answer to the client's problem. What was needed was their firm of "Generalists, Inc." who could look objectively at a business problem with a perspective unclouded by preconceived answers. You'll find a great example of this in Chapter 7 with the solution that Gossage proposed to German publisher Hubert Burda.

entertained thoughts similar to some of his own offbeat notions, he became as ecstatic over this serendipitous discovery as a welfare recipient who had just picked up a hundred dollar bill on a windy street."[25]

If David Ogilvy could end his *Ogilvy on Advertising* (1983) listing six advertising men as his mentors then we can assume that the polymath Gossage would instead have cited philosophers, physicists and theologians. And, judging from the unique style of advertising that Gossage ultimately created, numbered high amongst them would have been the mathematician, Norbert Wiener.

Meet the Father of the Information Age

At this juncture it's worth pointing out that Gossage was not alone in being influenced by Norbert Wiener. As his biographers Flo Conway and Jim Siegelman say in *Dark Hero of the Information Age* (2005), "He is the father of the information age. His work has shaped the lives of billions of people."[26] You are undoubtedly one of them and should, indeed, think of Norbert Wiener next time you get in the loop by logging into Facebook, or ask your boss, colleagues or friends for feedback.

Back in the pre-Facebook 'fifties, these terms, "getting in the loop" and "feedback", were already common parlance for scientists and civilians alike. As James Harkin, author of *Cyburbia* (2009) explains, the theory that produced them – cybernetics – was all the rage amongst "intellectuals, artists and all sorts of ordinary people who began to re-imagine society upon cybernetic lines and imagine that they were seeing cybernetic loops all over the place. This became what contemporary internet gurus now call a 'meme', a very viral idea which suddenly spread around post-war society and became a great way of understanding everything from the way a human holds a glass of water to the way the American post-war military machine was trying to understand its operations internationally."[27]

As an intellectual, an artist and, let's not forget, a businessman, Gossage would have seen its potential. In fact, we know he was familiar with cybernetics because of his reference to Wiener's *The Human Use of Human Beings* (1950) in his own writings. It is, however, in Gossage's description of his very distinctive approach to creative that the influence of Wiener's ideas about feedback and information loops becomes most obvious.

However, before we explore the impact those ideas had on Gossage, and other key figures we'll encounter in the coming chapters, let's take a closer look at Norbert Wiener and the ideas that so galvanised post-war America.

Getting in the loop with Norbert Wiener

It was during World War II that, according to Conway and Siegelman, the Massachusetts Institute of Technology Professor Wiener "conceived, defined, and quietly announced the coming of a new unified science of communication."[28]

It came about after this son of Russian Jewish immigrants volunteered to help in the war effort against Nazi Germany and began working on a way of helping anti-aircraft gunners predict the manoeuvring of German bombers in the night sky. What resulted was the "Statistical Predictor", a system for coordinating the action of man and machine which was predicated upon the constantly changing feedback that came from an information loop linking plane and pilot with gun and gunner.

Once World War II was over, Wiener despaired at the destructive purposes to which his ideas were being put, and determined to find a more benign use for cybernetics. He became convinced that the only hope for mankind lay in applying his theory to a new system of communication in which continuous feedback and instruction loops would enable individuals and groups to identify mistakes, rectify them and improve their performance and behaviour.

In short, "being in the loop", as it came to be known, meant playing an active role in society by remaining sensitive to the consequences of one's actions, and the responses and needs of others.

Nowadays it is hard to believe that a complex, even difficult, read like Wiener's first book *Cybernetics; or, Control and Communication in the Animal and the Machine* (1948) could become a bestseller. But as Conway and Siegelman say, "The book flew off the shelves. *Cybernetics* went through five printings in its first six months." [29]

In accounting for this success, Professor Fred Turner author of *From Counterculture to Cyberculture* (2006) explains, "We tend to forget that in the 1940s and 1950s, intellectual, academic culture was not nearly as cut off from public culture as it is today. Experts were published figures. Scientific experts, after all, were the ones who had won the war. So Norbert Wiener was very much a public figure in the wake of WWII ... and remained a public figure through to the 1960s."[30]

His celebrity was assured when he was lionised in *Time* and *Newsweek*. After that, as Conway and Siegelman point out, "Wiener's portly frame and prognostications were featured regularly in full-page photospreads in *Life*. His work became the subject of long articles in *Fortune*, *The New Yorker*, and a *Time* cover story on computers .... Cybernetics, feedback and the unwieldy name Norbert Wiener had become household words in America ...."[31]

In academic circles, his influence was immense. Bertrand Russell, who was reading Wiener's second book *The Human Use of Human Beings* at much the same time as an awe-stuck Howard Gossage came to call in 1952, described it as "a book of enormous importance."[32] Others were equally impressed. Wiener's theory informed the work of anthropologist Margaret Mead, neuroscientist Warren McCulloch and computer pioneer John von Neumann. It also had a massive impact upon an obscure English Professor at the University of Toronto, but we'll get to him in Chapter 5.

The new way to manufacture, manage – and advertise

It wasn't just academics who became avid cybernauts. American industry was also converted. If cybernetics was the precursor to such phenomena as artificial intelligence, robotics, prosthetics and computer-aided design then it also had a more immediate impact. Engineers adopted Wiener's electronic feedback devices and servo mechanisms to produce the washing machines, cookers, fridges and other consumer durables that turned the affluent American's home into what *Time* magazine called "the push button cornucopia."[33]

From factory floor to head office, Professor Turner points out, cybernetics "became the dominant working language of American industry. Systems Theory became the norm across a number of different disciplines. The American business world was in love with the idea that you manage a system. What should a manager do but seek 'feedback' and act on the basis of 'feedback' by doing some 'active listening'? We take these for granted now but they are all essentially cybernetic concepts."

The ramifications for one the US's most thriving post-war industries, advertising, were potentially huge. As Professor Turner continues, "Norbert Wiener's cybernetic information theory was different from many ways we think about communication. Most see it as a 'Sender', 'Message', 'Medium', 'Receiver' process. So a person has an idea, they turn it into words, they send it out to you via a medium and then you change your actions based upon their words. That's a mode of communication that has driven advertising for a long time. Norbert Wiener had a very different understanding. To Norbert Wiener, communication was a process of interaction. I send something out to you, you in turn send something back to me, your response in turn triggers another communication and we go forward together, doing things together. That's Norbert Wiener's vision, and it's a very different one from the more instrumental kind that we tend to think of as defining communication."[34]

As far as advertising was concerned it was, indeed, very different — especially when you consider that Rosser Reeves's Sender/Message/Medium/Receiver approach to delivering the USP was the dominant practice of the time.

As we've seen, Gossage rejected that theory as wasteful and irresponsible. And, after an exhaustive search for a more humane alternative, created his own approach that applied all of Wiener's precepts to the practice of marketing communication.

Here he is explaining that approach: "We can do one ad at a time. Literally, that's the way we do it. We do one advertisement and then wait to see what happens; and then we do another advertisement. Oh, sometimes we get way ahead and do three. But when we do, we often have to change the third one before it runs. Because if you put out an advertisement that creates activity, or response, or involves the audience, you will find that something has happened that changes the character of the succeeding ads."[35]

Or, as he told *Advertising Age* in March, 1959, "If you say something as interestingly as you can, you can then expect the other party to make a response. So the next time run a new ad; develop the dialog. It makes the conversation much more interesting. And rewarding."[36]

He put it even more succinctly when he said the agency's technique "consists of planting an idea through an ad and then waiting to see what happens before doing another ad."[37]

It all sounds very simple but what Gossage was describing in that sentence was an approach to advertising that no one else was to attempt for another 35 years.

Which gave him quite a head start on everybody. Let's see how he used it.

Chapter 4

INVENTING INTERACTIVE IN THE 1950s

(AND THE ADVERTISING/PR EVENT IN THE 1960s)

"NEVER CONFUSE
THE MESSAGE
WITH THE PRODUCT"

When Howard Gossage said, "You do one ad and see what happens; then you do another", he was explaining 'Cybernetics 101; Advertising Module'.[1] The only thing is, as we saw at the end of the last chapter, he was so far ahead of his time it would be another two generations before anyone else signed up for the course.

Undaunted, using the language of cybernetics, he went on to say, "Every action has an equal and opposite reaction; there is feedback in every ad. Some of it doesn't amount to much and some of it is negative, but it is there all the same."[2]

If, as Norbert Wiener asserted, feedback is a method of controlling a system by reinserting into it the results of its performance then, to Gossage, the adman and the audience were linked via one inclusive information loop, and the feedback that came round that loop enabled the adman to write ever more interesting and involving communications.

Just as Wiener saw this constant modification of the message as a means of making the world a better place, then according to advertising chief Jeff Goodby, so too did Gossage: "Gossage was certainly influenced by information loops and the whole theory that things went out and came back and went out and came back to you, and I think that's what he tried to exploit. And in a way I think it was a way of overcoming the loneliness of modern times ... I think he wanted to overcome that. I think he wanted to use media to connect with people and hear what they had to say and to tell them things, and to have a conversation with them instead of just talk *at* them."[3]

This approach differed from the two conventional ways of putting together an advertising campaign. The first, which owed much to Rosser Reeves, entailed devising a simple advertising expression of the product's USP, block booking time slots on TV or radio, and then repeating the commercial until it eventually registered in the audience's consciousness.

The second was more applicable to Gossage's preferred medium, press advertising. It would begin with the agency creating a series of press advertisements that collectively communicated the product's primary benefit. These would be presented to the client *en bloc*. If the client bought this campaign then the agency would run the ads either simultaneously or in sequence over the coming three, six or 12 months.

Either way, both imposed their messages upon the public with little allowance for how the receiver might think or feel. They were simply expected to act on the messages projected by the ads. And if that took ten or more viewings then so be it.

Waiting for feedback

By inviting his readers into the communication loop, Gossage was avoiding either approach. As he said, ours "runs counter to the usual procedure of preparing a whole year's campaign in advance which, of course, is a much more convenient way to do it, but commits you to more or less static advertising."[4]

This waiting for feedback put Gossage under extreme pressure. As his wife Sally recalls, "He was always under the gun because he didn't write a whole campaign ahead or anything like that. He'd get inspired to write one piece, and he would wait and see what the response was. But it always came and it always fed him, and he would be up all hours fashioning the next one."[5]

Gossage felt it was worth the effort. To him, advertising wasn't static, it was dynamic. It wasn't a statement, it was a dialogue. And it certainly wasn't to be passively consumed by some distant target audience, it was designed to be acted upon.

What's more, not only did Gossage's believe it was wasteful to blindly transmit your messages with no real sense of who was receiving them and how they were being received, he also saw feedback in ethical as well as commercial terms. In an interview with the *Kansas City Star* he explained, "I will go further and say that it is not only wrong to attempt to influence an audience without involving it but it is unethical and dishonest."[6]

Here, in his talk of ethics and honesty, we might again see parallels with Norbert Wiener. As we've noted above, the mathematician devised his theory as a means of ameliorating mid-twentieth century man's situation. He saw the creation of information loops as beneficial and, indeed, life-enhancing ways of making people respect others and accept responsibility for their own behaviour.

Gossage had come to the conclusion that there was little that was life-enhancing about the vast majority of Madison Avenue's output. He also despised the lack of respect that those hectoring advertisements displayed for their audience.

He was determined to be different and, using information loops and feedback, devised a whole new style of advertising. According to Jerry Mander, "Gossage had a term for it. He called it 'interactive'."[7]

Interactive advertising in the analog age

In so doing, Gossage had coined that term 40 years before it became the conventional way to describe digital communications. But how then did he do interactive in an analog age?

Answer: The humble coupon.

Now, at this point, some of you might say "Aha, so Gossage was a direct marketer." Well yes, definitely. But no one was writing lead-generation press ads like those created by Gossage. Couponed ads were the province of the mail order companies, and they used a form of hard sell that would have made Rosser Reeves blanch. There was certainly never any consideration for the impact their advertising might have on either their reader's sensibility or the image of the brand they were promoting.*

Gossage, on the other hand, was using his coupons to build a rapport between the reader and the brand. Jeff Goodby describes this very early form of what is nowadays termed brand response when he says, "He put coupons on all his press ads, even if it wasn't necessary to have one. He'd put one in that said 'we're not expecting you to buy anything, just write to us some time and tell us how things are going'. That was a coupon! And he would spring off of things that people wrote in and write another ad that said 'Bob from Dallas just wrote to us . . . .' He would make an ad out of the last thing that happened. It was very interactive and very much like what happens on the internet."[9]

Jerry Mander agrees: "He used the coupon much more than anyone else for this kind of interaction. It wasn't always to buy something. In fact, it was rarely about buying. It usually had some kind of exchange so the reader would feel they were closer and more engaged with the author."[10]

---

*That was true even of the man who introduced the term "direct marketing" in 1961 and gave the discipline a semblance of sophistication, Lester Wunderman. Creative, as Gossage knew it, was not his concern. In fact, according to his memoirs *Being Direct* (2004) his biggest contribution on that front was the introduction of the FSI (Freestanding Insert) – the bumf that drops out of your magazines as you're walking up to the counter to pay for them.[8]

There was another way in which he made the reader feel closer to the author. As Jerry Mander continues, "He viewed advertising less as a commercial bludgeon and more as a conversation between equals".[11] The man himself felt that the secret lay in developing a writing style that was genuinely conversational. As he told *Advertising Age* in March 1959, "Most ads come out with the same sort of personal tone you might manage to achieve when you're talking to your wife while other people are in the office."[12] For his advertisements, Gossage tried to write as if he really was sitting opposite his reader and talking with them — and them alone.

Taking the conversation some place interesting

Gossage told Jerry Mander that there was one final way of getting the reader to engage with the advertisement: "Never confuse the message with the product".[13] By that he meant that while the advertisement might be *for* a certain product, it wasn't necessary for the ad to be *about* that product. Yes, the aim was to ultimately sell it but that could come about via a circuitous route.

Actually Gossage didn't see it as circuitous. He saw himself as building "parallel structures". As Jerry Mander recalls, "If you're entering into a conversation with the reader and you need to talk about a product, Gossage said it is better to take the conversation over to the side and get the reader engaged in another conversation. Once you've got them involved only then should you bring them back to the product. That's the thing he did very often, starting a conversation over there and tying the link right at the end."[14]

That's not to say that Gossage used that most heinous of advertising tricks, borrowed interest i.e. getting the prospect's attention by showing something unusual or startling that is unrelated to the product that is being sold. In all his work, the idea that drove the conversation was germane to the product — it's just that Gossage rarely made the connection obvious enough for the reader to realise that they were being sold to.

But "sold to" they were. As Jerry Mander points out, "It always had a commercial intent. That is to say, the idea had to acquaint the reader with something about the product or, at the very least, the point of view of the advertiser".[15]

And, according to Gossage, it worked: "People like to be treated as human beings rather than as consumers, and they react very well to it, particularly when it comes to trotting down to the store, gas station or saloon and buying some. Every one of our clients has enjoyed notable sales increases."[16]

Interactive in action

One of the best examples of treating people like humans rather than consumers came when the brilliant publisher of *Scientific American* magazine, Gerard Piel, asked Gossage if he would write a campaign aimed at getting big-spending airline companies to advertise in the magazine's pages.

The usual product-focused response would have been to run a headline and visual that drew attention to the number of frequent air travellers who read *Scientific American* – thus promising the airlines a lucrative audience for their advertising. The copy would then have supported this assertion via statistics about the readers' astronomical average income, and their taste for frequent and luxurious air travel.

But as Jerry Mander says, "Howard's approach was not the usual one. He came up with the '1st International Paper Airplane Competition'. We gave prizes in four different categories. One was for 'Distance Flown', another was 'Time Aloft', the third was 'Aerobatics' and the fourth was 'Origami'. We had a board of judges that included the skydiving champion of the world, and held the final 'Fly-off' in the New York Hall of Science." [17]

If Gossage's response to the brief was unusual so, too, was his approach to the creative work.

Dugald Stermer was the art director on the press advertisement that launched the competition and he recalls, "The first ad was in *The New Yorker* and there was too much copy for the size of type that I wanted to use and I said 'can we cut a little bit of copy?' And he said, 'It's still a little tight.' So I said, 'OK, let's buy the back page on the reverse of the ad so that people can tear the page out and make an airplane out of it.' And we bought a whole advertising page just for that one paragraph of copy. Isn't that brilliant? I said, 'You're not serious. You're not really going to do this?' But Gossage had the power to persuade them."[18]

It may have seemed unorthodox, but there was method to all this madness. In fact, what we see here is one of Gossage's classic parallel structures. For, having started

[Scientific American Calls For Entries: Can It Be There's A Paper Plane Which Makes The SST 30 Years Obsolete?]

1st International Paper Airplane Competition

Scientific American primarily concerns itself with what Man is up to these days, and our readership is known for travelling more than that of any other magazine. So it is little wonder we have spent considerable time studying the two designs for the supersonic SST airplane recently announced by Boeing and Lockheed. (See Fig. 1 and Fig. 2.)

Soon we'll all be flying around in thin air at Mach 2.7, i.e., from New York to London in 150 minutes. Quite a prospect!

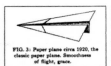

FIG. 3: Paper plane circa 1920, the classic paper plane. Smoothness of flight, grace.

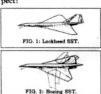

FIG. 4: First developed among paper airplane designers in the 1930's. Known for spectacular darting motions. Note hooked nose.

We do not mean to question the men at Boeing and Lockheed, or their use of traditional forms. But it seems to us unjust that several million paper plane designers around the world are not also given their due, a credit which if it had been extended some years ago would have saved the pros quite some straining at the drawing boards.

Well anyway, with design having caught up with itself, we can now postulate that there is, right now, flying down some hallway or out of some moviehouse balcony in Brooklyn, the aircraft which will make the SST 30 years obsolete. No?

Consider this: Never since Leonardo da Vinci, the Patron Saint of paper airplanes, has such a wealth of flight

FIG. 1: Lockheed SST.

FIG. 2: Boeing SST.

Still, at the close of our inquiry there remained this nagging thought: Hadn't we seen these designs somewhere before?

Of course. Paper airplanes. Fig. 3 and Fig. 4 illustrate only the more classical paper plane designs, in use since the 1920's or so, having a minimum performance capability of 15 feet and four seconds.* (See over)

research and experimentation remained untouched by cross-disciplinary study and publication. Paper airplane design has become one of those secret pleasures performed behind closed doors. Everybody does it, but nobody knows what anyone else has learned.

Many's the time we've spied a virtuoso paper plane turn the corner of the office hallway, or suddenly rise up over

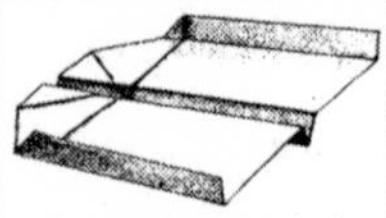

FIG. 5: Drawn from memory, this plane was last seen in 12th floor stairwell at 415 Madison Avenue. Do you know its designer? Where is he?

the desk, or on one occasion we'll never forget, veer first down the stairs to the left, and suddenly to the right, staying aloft 12 seconds in all. (See Fig. 5.)

But who is its designer? Is he a Board Chairman or a stock boy? And what has he done lately?

All right then. In the interests of filling this information gap, and in light of the possibility that the future of aeronautics may now be flying in a paper plane, we are hereby calling for entries to the 1st International Paper Airplane Competition.

The copy for the advertisement that launched the 1st International Paper Airplane Competition was too long to fit on the page so, instead of cutting it, Gossage persuaded the client to buy the reverse page, too. This enabled him to run the ad as intended, and the reader to tear out the page and use the paper to make their own airplane.

an interesting conversation over in one place, he made sure that he tied it all back to the product. As a *Business Week* profile explained: "Buried in the text were off hand references to *Scientific American's* subscribers 'who fly so much' and to their habit of travelling more than others. If the thumping response to the contest is a reliable sign, commercial airlines will get the message and begin advertising to those well-travelled subscribers."[19]

It was, and they did. By 11.00am on the day of the launch, Gerard Piel had had calls from Eastern Airlines and American Airlines placing advertising in his magazine. The latter also asked permission to run its own in-flight paper airplane contest, and provided instructions, entry forms and paper for its passengers to work on their prototypes whilst airborne.

And that was just the beginning. The launch advertisement ran once in only three publications: the *New York Times*, *The New Yorker* and *Travel Weekly*, yet the feedback was immense. As Gossage himself declared, "There were over 11,000 entries from 28 countries. The *New York Times* found it all entrancing as did the *LA Times*, *Der Spiegel*, *Time*, *Newsweek*, and our own dear old *San Francisco Chronicle*, and the radio and television networks."[20]

The interest didn't stop there. For, as we'll see later, the aim of what Gossage called his "ad platform technique" was always to amplify the original advertising message via a variety of media. In this case, the massive press interest began the amplification. It then grew with the toyshop FAO Schwarz introducing a line of elaborate paper airplanes created by industrial designer and husband to Alice, Lewis Lowe. And it culminated in *The Great International Paper Airplane Book*. The latter had sold 10,000 copies even before publication and went on to be a bestseller. Which meant that months and even years after the original advertisement had appeared, Gossage's idea was still being talked about and *Scientific American* was still getting calls from prospective advertisers. All for an estimated media spend of $40,000.

Gossage v Ogilvy

Campaigns like these confirmed Gossage's reputation as a maverick. To see just how different he was, let's compare his interactive approach to that of that other late starter in the advertising business, David Ogilvy.

Ogilvy is often cited alongside Bill Bernbach as firing the first shots of the creative revolution that swept through the industry in the 'sixties. Both Ogilvy and Bernbach were great creative directors. Their leadership styles were, however, very different. While Bernbach was happy to oversee his department and coax brilliant work from his art director and copywriter teams, he rarely took a brief himself and hated writing body copy. Ogilvy, on the other hand, wrote every word of all the famous advertisements which established his agency's creative reputation.

Like Gossage, Ogilvy specialised in press advertising and, more specifically, in writing what today would be known as long copy. For example, for one advertisement on behalf of The World Wildlife Fund he wrote 3,232 words.

Unlike Gossage, however, Ogilvy was convinced that the product should be the absolute focal point of the advertising. And he would dig deep to find the facts that made it so. For example, in his biography he proudly recalled, "For Shell I created a campaign which, for the first time in the history of the oil industry, explained the *ingredients* of petrol" (Ogilvy's italics).[21]

Gossage also had a petrol account, the Dallas-based Fina company. As he explained, he did all the exhaustive research he needed to do in order to conclude that every brand of petrol was identical to every other brand of petrol. And no amount of product-based puffery could establish any kind of real competitive advantage.

So, instead of foisting some spurious magical additive upon the public, he decided to differentiate Fina by making them likeable, and did so with an advertisement that was the antithesis of the hard-sell approach of the competition.

Its headline read, "If you're driving down the road and you see a Fina station and it's on your side so you don't have to make a U-turn through traffic and there aren't six cars waiting and you need gas or something please stop in."

Not only did he present this advertisement to the client, but he also suggested that, thereafter, it become the strapline which appeared under the logo on every advertisement that Fina ran.

It's pretty safe to say that no one had ever written a headline – or a strapline – like it. Nor, in a category in which bombast ruled, had they ever been so disarmingly light-hearted and endearingly honest. Yet, in so doing, Gossage had claimed the high ground for Fina. And from that vantage point, he set out to lampoon those competitors' advertisements which talked up the magical properties of their product.

Pink Air

As Gossage told the client, there were no magical ingredients. In fact, in his opinion the last great marketing breakthrough had come twenty years earlier when gas stations started making some effort to clean their toilets. Other than that, the stuff that came out of the pump was a bog-standard commodity.

However, if Fina couldn't offer a magical additive to add to the other additives in its petrol, then it could put something special in the air that customers pumped into their tyres. At Gossage's wife Sally's suggestion, he proposed that that special something be "Pink Air".[22]

The launch advertisement announced the wondrous breakthrough; another ad offered a free pink balloon in lieu of a sample of pink air; while a third ad explained the massive nationwide pipeline that would be built to deliver the pink air to all Fina's 2,000 stations over the coming five years.

Such a spoof on standard marketing strategy cried out for a spoof line extension. So Gossage proudly announced the introduction of "Pink Asphalt". And, this being a Gossage campaign, there was a competition which people could enter in order to win 15 yards of pink asphalt, and a follow up advertisement announcing "Mother of five wins 15 yards of pink asphalt."

David Ogilvy, with his masterful command of the ingredients of petrol, would have frowned on such work for it broke #13 of his rules on how to do advertising, "Humorous copy does not sell".[23] The public, however, enjoyed them. And so did the client, Jack Shea, who showed his appreciation by increasing his fee to become the agency's biggest account. It was money well-earned, for Gossage's work helped Shea expand the number of Fina Stations from 500 to 3,200 throughout the Midwest and Southwest.[24]

Gossage had similar success with another rule-breaking campaign. This one was for Eagle Shirts and it, too, bears direct comparison with Ogilvy's finest work.

[*OUR MOTTO*]*

"IF YOU'RE DRIVING DOWN THE ROAD AND YOU SEE A FINA STATION AND IT'S ON YOUR SIDE SO YOU DON'T HAVE TO MAKE A U-TURN THROUGH TRAFFIC AND THERE AREN'T SIX CARS WAITING AND YOU NEED GAS OR SOMETHING** PLEASE STOP IN."***

* We know it isn't very pushy as mottos go, but it's realistic and Fina doesn't expect you to do anything that isn't reasonable or convenient.

** Like oil. And 150% other items your car might need.

*** Meanwhile, if you're missing a valve cap (and you probably are) and would like a pink one we will be happy to send you one free and post paid. Just fill out the coupon. If you'd also like a Fina credit card application just put an X in the right box.

------------| COUPON |------------

American Petrofina, Dallas, Texas

Dear Fina:

☐ Please send me a Pink Valve Cap.
☐ Please send me a Fina Credit Card Application.

Name_____ Address_____

City_____ State_____

© 1962, AMERICAN PETROFINA, DALLAS, TEXAS

FINA

It's safe to say that no one had ever written a headline — or a strapline — like this one. Nor, in a category in which bombast ruled, had they ever been so disarmingly light-hearted and endearingly honest. Note the Fina Credit Card that was being offered in the coupon (there was a selling message in all Gossage's ads) and the Pink Valve Cap (there was always an effort to involve the reader and create a community.)

[*FINA STAKES OUT ITS CLAIM TO THE ADDITIVE OF THE FUTURE.*]

PINK AIR!

The following news item appeared in the San Francisco *Daily Commercial News* for March 21st, 1961:

Gasoline service stations will be filling your tires with tinted or brightly colored air in the foreseeable future, according to R. G. Lund, marketing consultant.

Detecting a strong trend in the industry, Lund said, "The oil companies are already adding additives to additives in their efforts to win motorists' favor in this highly competitive field. They have added extra ingredients to everything connected with an automobile except the air that goes in the tires. An additive for air will definitely be the next major advance."

It will take ten years, the Portland, Oregon marketer estimates, before the research and manufacturing problems are solved. Existing facilities will have to be converted to meet the public's demand for more colorful presentation of products. "But then," he concludes, "stations will feature air in decorator shades of green, blue, purple and even pink."

A word to the wise if we ever saw one. Fina's not the kind of company that has to be told twice. Pink sounds like as good a color as any and besides it's short and catchy. This is to serve notice we have settled on Pink Air.

Not only that, but as of right now we are starting a crash program: the Fina Five Year Plan. If it is going to take everybody else ten years we'll do it in half the time.

So look for Pink Air at the thousands of Fina stations on May 12th, 1966! Give or take a few days.

The reason we're in such a rush is, as the man says, if you want to stay on top you've got to have a little something new from time to time.

But Fina's gas, oil, and accessories are already just exactly as good as the best. We wouldn't want to add more things to them just so we could say we did. (Oh, we've got additives, all right, we just can't think of any good names or numbers for them.)

And that's why we're so pleased to have a brand new additive of our very own: Pink Air. If you see anybody else claiming it, just let us know and we will deal with them for sure. Keep your eyes open.

Meanwhile we'd like to be able to give you a better idea of what the air in your tires will look like on P.A. Day, May 12th, 1966. And right now we're trying to make up a few experimental batches of Pink Air. By the time our next ad comes out we'll be able to mail you a sample if we can just figure how to keep it from leaking out of the envelope.

Now, before we go here is a picture of our Fina emblem:

...so the next time you see a Fina station you'll recognize it. And if it's on your side so you don't have to make a U-turn and there aren't six cars waiting and you need gas or something, please stop in.

©1961, AMERICAN PETROFINA, DALLAS, TEXAS

While most other petrol brands talked up their magical ingredients, Gossage lampooned them by introducing Fina's new additive: pink air for the customer's tyres.

[*A PEEK AT PREMIUM PINK, THE ADDITIVE OF THE FUTURE*]

SEND FOR YOUR FREE
SAMPLE OF PINK AIR!

(As we know, there is a strong trend in the gasoline station industry toward adding a coloring ingredient to the air which goes into your tires. Like blue, purple, green, crimson, and others. The reason is: additives have been added to everything else connected with your car. Now it is air's turn. But authorities estimate that it will be ten years before the switchover from ordinary air is completed and colored air is in the hoses.

Meanwhile Fina, an alert young oil company, has staked out Pink Air! And has started a crash program so they can beat everybody else by five years: the Fina Five Year Plan.)

WE are happy to report some progress. Our Pink Air Research Laboratory at Mount Pleasant, Texas is hard at work on the secret ingredient which will turn air pink. We are still confident that we will be able to get it to our more than 2,000 Fina stations by May 12, 1966. About 4:30 P.M., we figure; some of our trucks don't get around until late in the afternoon.

We will keep you posted.

However, a technical question has been brought to our attention: "How is anybody going to know what Pink Air looks like when it's inside a tire?"

That is a good question and to answer it we will send you a sample as we promised in our last ad. A Free sample.

Naturally, for security reasons* we won't be able to send you any *real* Pink Air. Besides, what would we mail it in? No, the best answer is a pink balloon,** so when you blow it up Regular air will look like Premium Pink.

And there'll be a Fina emblem on it so the next time you're driving down the road and you see it and the station is on your side so you don't have to make a U-turn and there aren't six cars waiting and you need gas or something, please stop in. And see for yourself that our products are just exactly as good as the best.

And when you're through looking at the Pink Air give it to the kids, they'll like it. How many children do you have?

*It might float into the wrong hands. Enough said.
**Actually, TWO balloons, one inside the other. Don't worry, we'll send directions.

Fina Pink Air Development Division
American Petrofina
Dallas, Texas

[**FREE PINK AIR COUPON**]

Dear Fina:

I would like to see what Pink Air looks like. I have _____ children.

Name _____ Address _____

City _____ State _____

©1965, AMERICAN PETROFINA, DALLAS, TEXAS

In typical fashion, Gossage got people to interact by offering them a free sample of pink air.

*FINA CONSIDERS THE LOGISTICS IN GETTING PINK AIR, THE ADDITIVE OF THE FUTURE,
TO LITTLE FINA STATIONS AS WELL AS BIG FINA STATIONS*

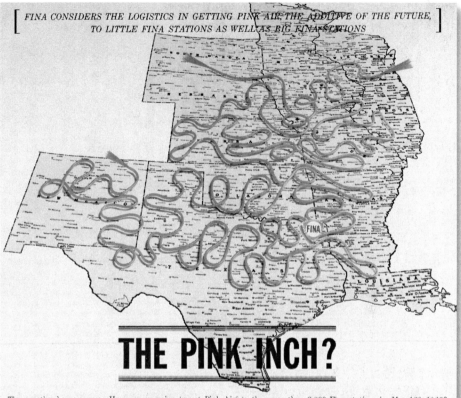

THE PINK INCH?

The question has come up: How are we going to get Pink Air to the more than 2,000 Fina stations by May 12th, 1966?

(Pink Air, if you recall, is Fina's additive of the future; the secret ingredient which will color the air in your tires. It is the only possible additive left; everything else in your car has already been taken care of. So Fina can be first, we have started a crash program, The Fina Five Year Plan.)

There are two answers:

1. That we transport Pink Air the same way we do our gasoline; from our refineries in Mount Pleasant, Wichita Falls, and El Dorado to distribution points where our trucks would pick it up and deliver it to Fina stations who would then put it in your tires. This is impractical because the pink air might mingle with and color the gasoline. Our gas doesn't need any more additives; it is already as good as the best and we wouldn't want to gild the lily — not even pink.

2. That we build a special pipe line for Pink Air: The Pink Inch. (See map above.) This isn't as easy as it sounds; it would be a lot of hard work and would probably cost a pretty penny. You know, you don't just get out there and lay pipe across the countryside. You've got to ask people's permission and pay them something to boot. Still, if we have to do it we have to do it.

Maybe the easiest thing would be to make it a hose line, out of air hoses like we use in our stations, only thousands of miles long. And a little bigger: The Pink Inch Hose Line. We don't suppose people would mind so much having a hose strung across their front yards except they might trip over it.

The real advantage to the proposed Pink Inch Hose Line is that it would be fair. It would make Pink Air available at the big Fina stations and the little Fina stations at one and the same time, without fear or favor.

[BIG FINA STATION]

[LITTLE FINA STATION]

A big Fina station has, in addition to lots of pumps you can see, lots of underground storage tanks; and lots of attendants to keep check on them. So taking care of Pink Air would be no problem at all to them.

But a little Fina station might be just two pumps in front of a general store and the proprietor not only has no extra storage space but is plenty busy as it is, what with slicing bacon and all. You might have to honk twice, not that he doesn't give you good service once he knows you're there. So you can see that a direct hose from the refinery would be a real help to him.

There are still a few details to be worked out in laying that much hose; such as how to get it across highways. Maybe when we come to a road we could string it between poles. If the telephone company people will cooperate. Well, we have five years to iron out the kinks and we'll probably need every minute of it.

Meanwhile, if you are driving down the road and you see a Fina station and it's on your side so you don't have to make a U-turn through traffic and there aren't six cars waiting and you need gas or something, please stop in.

(We've said this so often now that it's gotten to be sort of the Fina motto. It isn't very pushy as mottos go but it's realistic. We don't expect you to do anything that isn't reasonable or convenient.)

© 1961, AMERICAN PETROFINA, DALLAS, TEXAS

Gossage always played his wild ideas perfectly straight. Here he explained the infrastructure required to deliver the pink air (and subtly made the point about how big a player Fina was becoming in the West and Southwest).

[WE PAVE THE WAY FOR ANOTHER GIANT STEP IN THE FINA FIVE YEAR PLAN]

YOUR CHANCE TO WIN 15 YARDS OF PINK ASPHALT

PINK ASPHALT?

Why not? As you may remember Pink Air, Fina's Additive of the Future, was invented to make the insides of your tires look prettier because everything else that goes into your car already has all the extra additives it needs; sometimes more. And we started our Five Year Coach Program so as to be sure of getting it to all of our thousands of big and little Fina stations by Pink Air Day, May 11, 1966.

WELL you know how it is in a company when one department gets something special; it's like with kids. Right away the TBA* Department wanted a Pink Program too. So the Pink Valve Cap ("the accessory to help you through the difficult withdrawal period from Regular Air to Premium Pink") was invented.

Then somebody in Trucking said: "How about painting a few of our trucks pink so people will know we're ready to transport the Pink Air from our Fina refineries in case the Pink Air Pipeline** isn't completed by P.A. Day?" And so we did.

Meanwhile back in the Asphalt Department people were feeling Left Out. It isn't an ordinary little old stick-in-the-tar asphalt department, either; we are one of the country's big manufacturers of asphalt. And it is good stuff, sort of an asphalt man's asphalt. But only in basic black – until our boys made some revolutionary experiments.

Which is why we now have 15 yards of very high-quality Pink Asphalt to give away to the one who can think up the best way to use it. (15 yards is a whole heap of asphalt; pink or otherwise it weighs about 30 tons and, if you win it, it'll take us two double-dual wheel dump trucks or semi-trailers to haul it to your house.) After we roll it out for you, it'll cover around 270 square yards which is enough to pave a pink driveway plus a pink badminton court plus a pink patio. Or about ¾ths of a doubles tennis court? O.K., O.K., we'll pave the whole court.

Although nobody here knows how cows might feel about having their barn floor redone in wall-to-wall pink, we do know that asphalt is gentle on their feet; and neat. We suppose it would also be swell for paving sundecks on roofs; if only we can figure out how to get the steamroller up there. So if you happen to have anything you'd like paved for free with Premium Pink Asphalt just fill out part one of the coupon below and tell us what you want it for, and why. The best answer wins.

Meanwhile if you're driving down the road and you see a Fina station and it's on your side so you don't have to make a U-turn through traffic and there aren't six cars waiting and you need gas or something, please stop in.

* For Those Batteries Accessories; Fina stations sell several things besides gas and oil; hundreds.

** This is so complicated it took us a whole ad to explain it last time; but if you'd really like to know, just drop us a note and we'll be glad to send you a copy.

| PINK ASPHALT COUPON |

Pink Asphalt Department
American Petrofina
Dallas, Texas

Dear Fina:

○ Why I want 15 yards of Pink Asphalt is (you needn't limit yourself to 15 words or less. Use another piece of paper if you want):

□ While you're at it, I would like an application for a Fina Credit Card. I understand I can use it to buy any TBA item with no money down and six months to pay; is that right?

Cordially,

Name_____ Address_____

City_____ Zone____ State____

P.S. Also, while you're at it, you might as well send me one of your Pink Valve Caps, too.

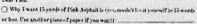

© 1965 AMERICAN PETROFINA, DALLAS, TEXAS

Such a spoof on standard marketing strategy cried out for a spoof line extension, so Gossage proudly announced the arrival of pink asphalt.

[FINA ANNOUNCES THREE IDENTICAL PRIZES
OR
IF A THING IS WORTH DOING IT'S WORTH OVERDOING]

MOTHER OF FIVE WINS 15 YARDS OF PINK ASPHALT

CONSOLATION PRIZE

GRAND PRIZE

SPECIAL PINK PRIZE

THE great Fina Pink Asphalt contest has ended in an unexpected three-way tie. We didn't say anything about what we do in case of ties so all three of the winners will each receive the Grand Prize, 15 yards of Pink Asphalt laid down where they want it. (This, you recall, is what the contest was about; to find the most interesting use for a batch of Pink Asphalt our asphalt division whipped up to match Pink Air – Fina's additive of the future coming May 12, 1966 – as well as our pink gas trucks, pink valve caps, etc.) The entries were so stimulating that the judges couldn't make up their minds, so we have had to scrape up an additional 30 yards to cover the other two winners.

GRAND PRIZE goes to Mrs. Bernie Rohling of 3407 Belmont Blvd., Nashville, Tennessee. This poses some problems, being outside our marketing area; we may have to smuggle the stuff to her. She says "For years I have been tying pink ribbons on bassinets, all to no avail. – I have five sons. Your contest has brought new hope into my life. How could old man stork miss leaving the right bundle if our house was plainly marked with 15 yards of beautiful pink asphalt driveway?" And she concludes, "Here's hoping, or should I say expecting?" Good luck, Mrs. Rohling!

Consolation Prize goes to Valley Center High School, Valley Center, Kansas – a new suburb of Wichita – 86 of whose students wrote rousing letters. Several wanted a pink tennis court. "Which we badly need," says one, "since there isn't a tennis court, or swimming pool, or park even in the whole town – yet." Another states: "We have done so poorly at football this year there must be *something* we can excel

in; maybe it is tennis." Still another: "The old school spirit at V.C.H.S. (established 1958) can't be beat. But we haven't ever done anything anybody has heard about. It is hard to brag under such conditions. A pink tennis court would make us famous. Also it would match the trim of our building, which is pink. Maybe we will even change the school colors from purple and gold to purple and pink." Four of the 86 thought they needed a pink drag strip more, however. Well, fight it out among yourselves and congratulations all!

A Special Pink Prize goes to Mr. W. H. Moseley of 3901 Sockwell Blvd., Greenville, Texas. We found Mr. Moseley's entry especially noteworthy since he happens to be a Fina dealer; the first known instance of a company man winning a contest; we forgot to make a rule against it. You may remember that one time we mentioned in an ad that not all Fina stations were big super-stations? That some Fina stations were more modest? Mr. Moseley's is one of them, but he is anxious to improve himself. He was about to repave his driveway when he heard of our contest. He has stalled off in the hopes that his could be the first Fina station paved pink; with the result that the drive is beginning to collect a bit of water in the wet weather while he waits to find out whether to go to pink or black. He ends on a somewhat familiar note, "Meanwhile if you are driving down the road and you see this station and it is on your side and there aren't six cars (or rowboats, if you don't hurry) waiting please stop by." So, congratulations to you, Mr. Moseley, and best wishes for a dry, Pink 1962!

Our sincere thanks to all of you who wrote in; we enjoyed the fun and we hope you did, too; and that we will hear from you again sometime.

© 1962, AMERICAN PETROFINA, DALLAS, TEXAS

And, this being a Gossage campaign, there had to be a competition which people could enter — and an ad announcing a lucky winner — or three.

The Man in the Hathaway Shirt ...

The Hathaway Shirts account was the making of David Ogilvy, for it was his first campaign that was a hit with both the public and his advertising peers. Ogilvy took the business in 1951 as, primarily, a showcase for his creative abilities. In fact, legend has it that Ogilvy agreed to do the work for next to nothing on condition that the advertising that he presented ran without alteration.

The advertisement that launched the campaign featured a distinguished, middle-aged gentleman wearing a Hathaway shirt. Nothing too special about that, you might think. But the genius lay in the slight embellishment that was added at Ogilvy's insistence. As he explained, "I happened to have some research which showed that a wonderful factor to have in the illustration of any advertisement was 'story-appeal'. So I thought of 22 different story-appeal elements to put in the photograph of the Hathaway shirts. The twenty-second of them was an eye patch. It turned out to be a good idea."[25]

The eye patch gave the aristocratic model, White Russian George Wrangell, a rakish, mysterious air and, in so doing, differentiated this advertising from all other contemporary clothing campaigns.*

David Ogilvy's creative reputation was made and "The Man in the Hathaway Shirt" – as the headline read – spawned a highly successful campaign. It also prompted Howard Gossage to do something very different to Ogilvy's image-led visual and product-focused copy.

... versus Miss Afflerbach

Actually, having said that, Gossage's work for Eagle Shirts was entirely product-focused but, because of the parallel structure that he devised, it just doesn't seem that way. Indeed, his most famous campaign for Eagle Shirts could be construed as a blatant

---

*Going back to Gossage's belief in the power of the extra-environmental man, he reckoned there was another thing that differentiated the campaign: David Ogilvy had brought an outsider's vision to American advertising. As Gossage said, "Commander Whitehead [the star of his Schweppes campaign] was certainly extra-environmental, and so was Baron Wrangell, the Hathaway man with the eye patch."[26] Gossage maintained that what Ogilvy had done, almost unconsciously, was invest all his best work with a dissonant Englishness.

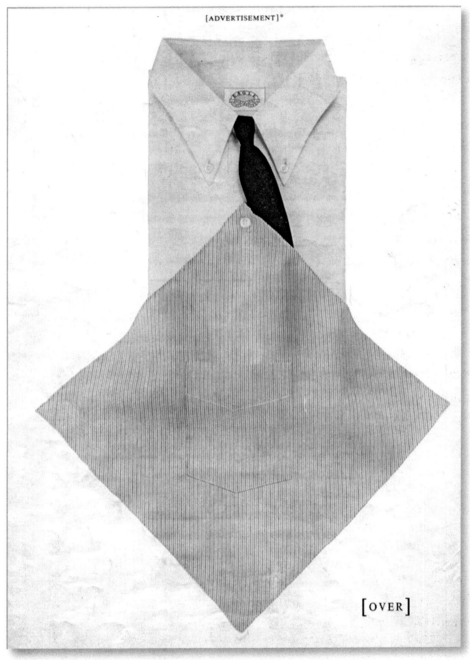

[ADVERTISEMENT]*

[OVER]

"Shirtkerchief" pulled the biggest response ever recorded for a single advertisement in The New Yorker...

[cont. from preceding page]

SEND FOR YOUR FREE EAGLE SHIRTKERCHIEF (SHIRTKIN?) (NAPCHIEF?)

AS far as we know this is a brand new invention. Perhaps you will be able to figure out how to realize its full potential. It all started when we tried to devise something to send you—short of an actual shirt—to illustrate a few of the fine points of fine shirt making. A sample to take with you when you go shirt shopping. So first we hemmed a piece of fine shirting; *20 stitches to the inch*, just like in our shirts. At this point you could still call it a handkerchief. But it did seem a shame not to show one of our threadchecked buttonholes, so we did. It makes a pretty good shirt protector: just whip it out of your breast pocket and button it on the second from the top to avoid gravy spots. Good. And tuck your tie in behind it. But then somebody in Pockets said, "Look, if you let us sew a pocket on it, it will show how we make the pattern match right across, no matter what." So if anyone knows what you can use a pocket in a handkerchief/napkin for we will be glad to hear. We will give a half-dozen shirts for the best answer. Make it a dozen.

Eagle Shirtmakers, Quakertown, Pa.

… but that was just the start, for it was always Gossage's aim to amplify the message delivered in the ad via a variety of media.

attempt to get the product into the prospect's hands, and starts out with that most conventional of ploys: the offer of a free sample which displayed the quality of both the cloth, the finishing and the stitching.

However, in the parallel structure being created by Gossage, this was no ordinary product sample. What he was offering the public was a square of shirt cloth with a buttonhole at one corner and a pocket at the centre. And what he was asking the public to do in the headline was "Send for your free Eagle Shirtkerchief (Shirtkin?) (Napchief?)".

After some musing in the body copy about what exactly the sample was, the advertisement concluded with a coupon which was to be returned to Miss Afflerbach at Eagle Shirts, and a question: "If anyone knows what you can use a pocket in a handkerchief/napkin for we will be glad to hear. We will give a half dozen shirts for the best answer. Make it a dozen."

As Alice Lowe reports, "The offer created the greatest reaction to a single advertisement which *The New Yorker* ever had" with over 11,000 people sending in their ideas.[27] Gossage was happy with the response, especially one assumes that of the correspondent who suggested using the pocket as a place in which to keep the black eye patch of the Man in the Hathaway Shirt.

Gossage was happy but not satisfied. For, as we saw in the 1st International Paper Airplane Competition, he always wanted the advertising message to be amplified by other media. And, sure enough, once sufficient well-written, witty and wacky responses had been collated, a book, *Dear Miss Afflerbach*, was launched to give Gossage's original idea new life – and Eagle Shirts thousands more new customers.

Well Red

There were more advertisements in the Hathaway Shirt campaign. All of which featured their visually impaired hero. And many of which promoted the range of colours and styles in which a Hathaway shirt might come.

Eagle were eager to promote their colour range, too. But, typically, Gossage took the parallel, interactive route. He knew that his erudite *New Yorker* audience were now in on the joke and, instead of doing advertisements about the extent of that range, he asked them for new shades and the names that might describe them. With tongue in cheek irony that he knew his readers would appreciate, he offered a grand prize of an all-expenses paid weekend in Eagle Shirts' Pennsylvania home town as the reward for the most imaginative name.

A later advertisement, featuring many of the suggested new colours, announced the winner. There was "Forever Amber", "Come Azure", "Hulla Blue", "Original Cinnamon", "Come and get me Copper", "Inalienable White", "Establish Mint", "Statutory Grape", "Dorian Grey", "Gang Green", "Medi Ochre", "Hi Ho Silver" and "Unforseeable Fuchsia".

As Alice Lowe recalls, "The press services promptly picked up the color name story resulting in hundreds of additional suggestions from every state in the Union .... The London *Times* ran the color name story and reportedly received 4,000 suggestions .... Years after the competition ended, people still sent in their color name suggestions."[28]

In fact, in 1969 the Ford Motor Company plagiarised the idea, announcing that its new model, the Maverick, would appear in such colours as "Thanks Vermilion", "Naval Orange" and "Freudian Gilt". Far from being offended by this bit of larceny, Gossage loved it. For it allowed him to mine even more PR from what had already been a very rich seam.

The master of PR – and the pseudo-event

Speaking of public relations, if Gossage was ahead of his time as regards interactive, he was also way out front with his understanding of the importance of managing the press. In fact, in developing the "ad platform technique" aimed at amplifying a marketing message, he was probably the first in the advertising industry to see the press and broadcast media as an integrated part of any communications plan.*

---

*By the end of the 'sixties, integrated work was the talk of the industry. But it wasn't the kind of integration that Gossage was pioneering. When, on 3rd February, 1969, *Advertising Age* ran the headline, "Integrated TV Ads Draw Praise of Admen" the story had nothing to do with combining different media into one strategy. It concerned "Commercials that integrate Negroes, Orientals and other minority group performers."

Gossage sometimes described his technique as journalistic, i.e. he always aimed to say something that was itself newsworthy. Here is how he explained it to his friend Barrows Mussey: "It took me a long time to discover just what the formula was. It is apparently this: that you can set forth a platform on a given subject, and have it exactly right word for word, through an ad, and then pursue the matter through press conferences and so forth with publicity."[29]

What Gossage was describing was what historian Daniel J. Boorstin had, in his controversial bestseller *The Image* (1961), termed a "pseudo-event". According to Boorstin, such synthetic happenings were flooding the media and blurring the line between real news and, what we now know as, marketing spin.

In defining a "pseudo-event", Boorstin could easily have been describing any one of Gossage's ideas: "It is planted primarily (not always exclusively) for the immediate purpose of being reported or reproduced. Therefore, its occurrence is arranged for the convenience of the reporting or reproducing media. Its success is measured by how widely it is reported."[30]

It was a method pioneered by Edward L. Bernays, the father of modern public relations, and was a much more effective form of marketing manipulation than any of Rosser Reeves's incessant thirty second commercials. Few admen, however, had understood its potential.

Gossage certainly regarded himself as having no competitors. As he said, "I am the only practitioner I know who does this on purpose. And I don't do it as often as I would like to."[31]

He realised that to do it more often, he needed help. Which is why, when he aligned with Jerry Mander in 1964, it wasn't only because of the young man's skills as a copywriter, but also for his talents as a publicist and PR specialist. As Jerry Mander recalls, "I came from public relations and was starting to do advertising and he saw that I was merging the two, and that was one of the things that got him interested in my participating with him. But he was doing it before I was doing it."[32]

He certainly was. As we saw in Chapter 1 with his 1949 campaign to feed the starving children of France, he instinctively understood the power of the media. At the very start of his career he was talking in terms of "successful propaganda" and saying, "Reality is not what happens but is controlled by what is written. We control the print and the air." The Nucoa margarine campaign is another early example of him developing the pseudo-event as news item. However, successful as they were, these and other of his earlier campaigns were small beer when compared to the massive media exposure he got for his work with the Seattle-based brewery, Rainier Ale.

Beer and Beethoven

It all started the day Gossage got a call from Al Levitt, who ran the local classical music station KSFR. Gossage, who loved classical music, was devastated to hear that Levitt had run out of money and was closing down. Desperate to help, Gossage reassured him that he'd persuade one of his clients, Rainier Ale, to advertise on the station. Rainier duly agreed to pick up the tab – and Gossage duly forgot all about it.

On the day the radio commercials were supposed to run, Gossage got a call from Al Levitt, who wanted to know where the commercials were and what they were about.

As Alice Lowe says "Of course, Howard could have just asked Levitt to extol the merits of Rainier Ale, but that would have been too prosaic a thing to do."[33] It would also have broken Gossage's rule about never "confusing the product with the message".

No. What he needed was an idea.

Now, they say that an idea is nothing more nor less than a new combination of old elements – and that the more old elements you have in your head, the more fertile your imagination. Well, as Gossage mused on the subject of an ale company advertising on a highbrow radio station he remembered a *Peanuts* cartoon he'd seen a year or so ago which featured a character wearing a sweatshirt with Beethoven's face on the front.

He conjured the stereotypical ale drinker in his sweatshirt down at the local bar watching the game on TV and imagined the same blue collar character at the classical concert. To cater to this clientele, he told Levitt that Rainer were now ready to offer them their very own Beethoven sweatshirts.*

---

*Gossage then called Charles M. Schulz, the creator of the *Peanuts* comic strip and originator of the Beethoven sweatshirt and offered to pay for usage rights, but Schulz was so pleased with Gossage's execution of the idea that he waived the fee.

Gossage followed up the Beethoven idea by trying to persuade Picasso to allow his prints to appear on a sweatshirt. It never happened, but it would have been another historic first.

This was another first, for until then sweatshirts carried either the name of a college or a fraternity house's initials. Never pictures. The Beethoven line was extended to include Bach and Brahms. There was even a community of KSFR listeners called "The Wolfgang Club" who insisted on a small run of Mozart sweatshirts being produced.

If overall demand was immense then, thanks to Gossage's prompting, so too was the coverage in the press. For, as the requests for the Beethoven sweatshirts came in, Gossage arranged for one to be delivered to the most famous conductor/composer in the US, Leonard Bernstein, who was soon pictured in the *New York Times* wearing his Beethoven sweatshirt whilst rehearsing with the New York Symphony Orchestra.

Alice Lowe recalls that "stories about the sweatshirts appeared in hundreds of newspapers and magazines .... Orders came from all over the United States and many foreign countries including England, Japan and Australia. Things became so hectic (orders had reached two hundred thousand), the agency finally had to put an end to handling the sweatshirt orders itself. It was either that or stop being an advertising agency."[34]

If that simple radio spot generated a hugely disproportionate amount of media noise then Gossage surpassed even that a couple of years later with perhaps his biggest PR coup of all.

The multi-million dollar advertising/PR event

It started when a frail-looking old man appeared at the Firehouse asking if there might be a chance of someone sponsoring him on a walk from San Francisco to the venue of 1962's World's Fair, Seattle.

The old man was actually a seasoned walker called John F. Stahl, and clearly he had the requisite stamina for both pounding the road and bearing a grudge. For, having been forcibly retired on disability from the US Postal Service in 1935, he'd dedicated his life to proving his former employers wrong by walking immense distances.

Gossage quickly recognised that Stahl's next proposed walk had great PR value to his Seattle-based beer client Rainier Ale, and set about writing the "ad platform" from which the press campaign could then be launched.

The advertisement was aimed at finding suitable travelling companions to accompany the sprightly old man. Of the several hundred who wrote in, three were invited to San Francisco to prepare for the trek – and to meet the press. Alice Lowe remembers, "Almost every day, one or another of the walkers was being interviewed by the local media and getting a fantastic amount of publicity for Rainier."[35]

Once the walk began, the interest intensified. Such was the coverage that a pleasantly surprised Gossage realised he had no need to write any advertisements. As he said, the media were doing the hard work for him: "The newspaper, television and radio coverage on the coast was enormous. Front page newspaper stories with pictures – sometimes five column pictures – and absolutely no reluctance to mention the client's name."[36]

Alice Lowe shared her boss's delight at the results of John F. Stahl's walk to Seattle, "The campaign was a stunning success. It resulted in four and a half months of free publicity in towns up and down the Pacific Coast; it enhanced Rainier's image, and boosted sales .... Again it proved Howard's thesis that effective campaigns need not cost a lot and that creativity should be paid its worth, not according to a media budget."[37]

It is difficult to put a monetary value on the free commercial airtime and column inches generated by this campaign, but it must have run into millions of dollars. All for what Alice Lowe calculated to be an out-of-pocket expense of $32,000.[38]

These shots were taken on the Golden Gate Bridge at the start of John F. Stahl's walk to Seattle. The occasion may seem pretty low-key, but remember Gossage's words: "Reality is not what happens but is controlled by what is written." And thanks to his masterful use of PR, the stunt generated millions of dollars worth of free publicity for the sponsor, Rainier Ale.

Once again it's worth saying how far Gossage was ahead of the game. It is only in the past ten years that similar PR-generating pseudo-events have become commonplace. Such is their popularity that they are an essential element of any campaign that aspires to a Grand Prix at the Cannes Advertising Festival. As such, every advertising student's book is now full of what they refer to as "stunts".

Rich Silverstein of Goodby, Silverstein & Partners explains the debt they owe to Gossage, "He was one of the fathers of this whole idea that you can make stunts. Right now, kids say 'you know, we could, er, dress up and do this thing at a bus shelter' and you're going 'OK, yeah, right'. But Howard was so brilliant, he did stunts 50 years ago."[39]

Tearing down the billboards

If, nowadays, people like Rich Silverstein see Gossage as a visionary, then back in the mid-'sixties his stance on advertising and the work he produced sometimes provoked a less favourable verdict.

Under a headline which described his advertising as "Crazy" one journalist wrote, "Gossage plays only his own particular brand of advertising, a wild one which takes place largely out of bounds." And concluded, "It is little wonder he is looked upon as an iconoclast by some of his peers, as a scoundrel by others."[40]

A profile in *Business Week* spoke of an even more estranged relationship: "Few projects he has set his hand and mind to make much sense to his rivals in the advertising business, to whom his name is anathema."[41]

Undeterred, and probably encouraged, by the attention he was getting for himself and his agency, Gossage continued what often seemed like a one-man campaign to change the industry.

Increasingly, however, that campaign changed its focus. If it started out as a fight against advertising that was banal, bombastic and boring, then it was developing into a crusade against the industry's irresponsibility and self-interest.

The latter found an early outlet in his stance against billboards. It came, in 1960, not in an advertisement but in an article in *Harper's* magazine.

As Gossage explained, most advertising hitched a ride on the back of such media as newspapers, magazines, radio and TV. It was the advertising's job to catch the audience's attention by being as interesting, if not more so, than the content around it. But, as he argued, in the case of billboards the content around it was the countryside or the cityscape. And no "media owner" had the right to sell that media because the view that the billboard was interrupting belonged to the people.

As intended, the article caused a furore. While representatives of the advertising industry accused him of betrayal, people who preferred scenery to slogans wrote in support, and the article ended up being read into the Congressional Record by Senator Maurine Neuberger of Oregon.

With the article in *Harper's*, and a subsequent campaign for Rover cars which asked readers to vote for and against billboards, Gossage was edging towards what would today be called an environmentalist position. And he was certainly to take a few steps further in that direction with his plans for the Irish Tourist Board.

Selling Ireland's whiskey …

He'd come to the Dail's attention with a low-budget campaign for a consortium of Irish Distillers. It was for them that he did one advertisement which outrageously stopped halfway through a sentence, and another ad the following week which picked up where the previous one had left off.

While one advertisement acquainted its American readers with the idea of Irish coffee made with a topping of whipped cream and a jigger of whiskey, another introduced them to the meaning of the Gaelic word "Flahoolik" – a "princely exuberance, a generosity or lavishness of spirit." Many who knew the author later applied that word to the man himself.

His Irish clients certainly enjoyed the craic he was creating, and the money it was making in extra sales. They'd also appreciated the way Gossage had, in 1959, moved to Ireland for a few months so he could bring the right flavour to his writing. In so doing he'd banished what he termed the "Disneyland of leprechauns, Mother Machrees, and paddywhackery" that characterised the American's view of the country.[42]

Now they eagerly awaited the ideas on promoting Irish tourism that might attract much needed dollars to the national exchequer. When he finally delivered his plan to the Irish government it amounted to a tourism campaign the like of which had not been seen before – or since.

STAND UP
& BE COUNTED!
ARE YOU PRIDE OR PROFIT?

[NUMBER III]

sides you'll probably be terribly anxious to receive your Pride Badge or your Profit Badge. one. For the benefit of you latecomers we [The Whiskey Distillers of Ireland] are referring to the very nice badges we are sending out from Dublin to all who write us here.

We unfortunately ran off the page last week and had to continue over. No harm done, we suppose. ☙ The badges, then, are as illustrated. "Profit" to be worn by those who glory in Irish Coffee and the money it sends flowing to Ireland. And a pretty thing it is, too, watching the dear sales curve course upwards thanks to the Profit Party's interesting taste. If bizarre. Not that we condemn, no, no, no. ☙ It's just that there are the others: the Prides; proud of the taste, proud of the altogether distinctive, burnished, but emphatic flavor of Irish Whiskey. They claim the subtlety is *quite drowned out* in Irish Coffee. Strong words! Strong feelings! Before we run out of space again perhaps we'd better get our coupon in. We are given to un-

Now this isn't to say that you must already be an all-outer for Irish Coffee or a practicing Irish Whiskey drinker to qualify as a Profit or Pride respectively. All we require is a willing heart and an open mind. Choose the side that appeals to you; state your allegiance and then justify it by deeds. If you change your mind

later write in and we'll send you the badge of whichever side you defected to. No recriminations, no sidelong glances, just understanding smiles is what you'll get from us. ☙ If you're a novice, though, this great, brilliant world of Irish Whiskey is likely to set you quite agog with its variousness. There are nine grand brands. It'll do no harm to list them [if you'll excuse us for a moment while we draw lots to see whose name shall go first]: Murphy's, John Power, Old Bushmills, Tullamore Dew, Paddy, John Jameson, Gilbey's Crock O' Gold, John Locke, and Dunphy's Original Irish. Now . . .

P.O. Box 186
Dublin, Ireland   [COUPON]
Pride [ ] Profit [ ] (indicate one)
Please send me a badge so that all may say
"There goes a (PRIDE), (PROFIT) man."

Name_____
Address_____
City_____State_____Country_____

---

derstand by those who know that a coupon [rather than just saying to write in] boosts the response tremendously. We hope this is true; so much advice nowadays is simply terrible.

Gossage's work for the Whiskey Distillers of Ireland had a particularly loyal following amongst The New Yorker's *sophisticated readers. In fact, Gossage developed such a rapport with them that he wrote one advertisement that finished half-way through a sentence and then ran this ad the following week, taking up the story where he'd left off.*

In another ad, he got 2,000 people to respond even though there was no offer and nothing to buy; they just wanted to get in touch. His own favourite in this campaign came when the distillers themselves visited New York. Gossage ran an ad saying they would be giving a party. Over 3,000 readers of The New Yorker *sent a coupon to Dublin requesting an invitation. Two hundred names were eventually drawn and they included the Mayor of New York, the Governor, the President of the United Nations and Cardinal Spellman.*

… and keeping out its tourists

To protect the country's culture and countryside from the anticipated tourist boom, Gossage suggested strictly vetting visitors. Not only did they need to be sensitive enough to appreciate the wonders of the place, their trip also had to enhance the lives and enrich the experience of their hosts. To this effect, Gossage drew up a list of occupations and enthusiasms against which any tourist would be checked. Those who got through would then be asked to pay a high admission fee.

Gossage figured that by adopting his suggestions, Ireland would not only be free of crass commercialism, but it would also become the most aspirational holiday destination on earth.

When it came to industrial development and the encouragement of inward investment, Gossage was just as protective of his adopted homeland. As Alice Lowe points out, "No tax free concessions would be made to factories offering employment in return for the right to poison the air, water and soil."[43]

Mr Sean Lemass, the Irish Prime Minister, liked the presentation. But he couldn't carry his colleagues with him, and Gossage's ground breaking approach to tourism was permanently shelved.

Again, when judged by today's standards, this approach would be called environmentalist. We can also see hints of the anti-globalisation which was to find much fuller expression in Gossage's 1967 campaign to free the Caribbean island of Anguilla. But more of that later. In 1960, no clearly defined sensibility existed for either ideology. Nor, in truth, was Gossage consciously adopting such positions. He was simply responding to what he saw as the shortcomings of conventional advertising and the commercialism it generated.

In the case of conventional tourist board advertising, he reckoned those shortcomings turned "everybody into slobs; both the inhabitants, who become venal, and scornful of the tourists, and the visitors, who become sort of sore-footed vandals who think the natives are … colorful, dirty extras posted around to pick their pockets."[44]

This, he maintained, was but one of many ways the industry abused its power. Looking back, Jerry Mander says, "He was increasingly angry about the one speaking to the many. The way advertising talked at people, pushed them around and bullied them."[45]

As we've seen, he responded by using information loops and feedback to devise a whole new way of communicating. One that, instead of pushing people around, put an arm round their shoulders and invited them to join him in conversation and even participate in writing the ads themselves. As Jeff Goodby says, "His idea was to ask 'what should I be saying to you? Write in, here's a coupon, write in and tell us what we should be telling you'." [46]

In promoting his interactive approach over conventional styles, Gossage anticipated the advocates of digital marketing who, 40 years later, would announce the death of the old-style advertising that "pushed" its messages at the public.

Back to the early 'sixties, however, and Gossage was a lone voice who, in his own words, was one of "those who have thought themselves into a sort of intellectual isolation, who lie awake and groan 'doesn't anyone else think like me?'"[47]

That isolation wasn't to last forever. And when rescue came it did so in the shape of a man who'd also been seized by the transforming effects of information loops and feedback. But this man had no intention of using them on something as transient as advertising. His aim was nothing less than the perfectibility of humankind.

This visionary was Marshall McLuhan, and it was Howard Gossage who took him from being an obscure Canadian academic to global celebrity and finally, as Gary Wolf, the executive editor of *HotWired* described him, "Electronic culture's immortal saint."[48]

Chapter 5

LAUNCHING
MARSHALL McLUHAN,
AND THE BIRTH
OF SOCIAL NETWORKS

"PLAY IT FAT, DUMB AND HAPPY"

Howard Gossage and Marshall McLuhan had much in common. Both were charismatic public speakers who delighted in saying contentious things, and then enjoyed the attention generated by the ensuing controversy.

Both were curious men with a passion for enquiry and discussion. This was probably inspired by the two being raised as Christian Scientists. As McLuhan's most recent biographer Douglas Coupland explains, back then it was "definitely not a Bible thumping denomination but a progressive way of being – much concerned with knowledge and debate and inquiry and communication and doubt."[1] Both men duly had their doubts and ultimately quit the church – Gossage becoming a very spiritual atheist and McLuhan a devout Roman Catholic.

Both men had almost total recall. However, while Marshall McLuhan was sometimes vague about his sources, Howard Gossage would happily attribute his own *bon mots* and big ideas to others.

Both men thought differently to their peers. Quite literally. McLuhan's brain was supercharged by not one but two carotid arteries at the base of his skull pumping oxygenated blood to his cerebral cortex. In similar vein, Gossage also benefited from an uncommon rush of blood. Like many long distance USAF bomber pilots in WWII, he was given handfuls of "go pills" to keep him awake and maintained this habit until, according to Alice Lowe, he "tossed them down as casually as if they were candy mints."[2]

Not that either man had much truck with the turned on, tuned in, dropped out drug culture of the 'sixties. Although both were sought out by the hirsute hippies they were, in terms of style and taste, conservative. Similarly, both men were simultaneously fascinated and troubled by the changes that were transforming the post-war world.

Which brings us to another crucial common denominator.

In the confusion brought by such changes both men, in their own fields, sought a way forward by adapting Norbert Wiener's cybernetic theory of communication and social organisation.

From understanding Wiener to *Understanding Media*

Stanford Professor Fred Turner says McLuhan was a great populariser of Wiener's ideas, and was indebted to them for his own fame. In *From Counterculture to Cyberculture*, Professor Turner says that McLuhan "drew extensively on the work of Norbert Wiener .... [and] was deeply influenced by the social role outlined in Wiener's 1950 volume *The Human Use of Human Beings*."[3]

James Harkin agrees. In his book *Cyburbia* he explains, "He had stumbled upon Wiener's book, *Cybernetics*, as early as 1950 and throughout the following decade ... tried to develop the theory of cybernetics to understand the evolution of modern literature. Such was McLuhan's enthusiasm for the subject that before long he had left behind the study of literature entirely in favour of a study of the information containers in which that literature was housed."[4]

This study of "the information containers" led McLuhan to pioneer, and in many ways invent, what is nowadays known as media studies. In the process, McLuhan became less interested in improving behaviour through the delivery of appropriate and timely messages, and more intrigued by the effect that the technology that sustained the information loops was having on society. And he concluded that that technology's impact on the individual was so consciousness-altering that the content that was being delivered was, in fact, irrelevant. As he famously put it, "The medium is the message."

It was a vision outlined in his 1964 book, *Understanding Media*. The subtitle, *The Extensions of Man* signposted McLuhan's other big idea. Drawing heavily on an unattributed Wiener and the cybernetics-influenced French Jesuit priest and philosopher Pierre Teilhard de Chardin, McLuhan asserted that electronic media were an extension of our central nervous systems. Not only that, because of the ubiquity of electronic media like TV, telephones and, to a lesser extent, radio they gave us a shared sensitivity and sensibility that cut across such barriers as nationality, geography and gender.

As James Harkin says, what McLuhan saw was "an electronic village in which each individual would be tied, via electronic cables, to a shared global consciousness."[5] Neurologically this would lead to nothing less than the reformation of human nature. The socio-economic impact would also be immense. Not only would old distinctions like race, class and caste be swept away but, as Harkin continues, for this new electronic tribe, the old world of "machinery and heavy industry would shortly give way to a society based around the flow of information through a kind of global network ...."*[6]

To the devoutly Roman Catholic McLuhan, this looked tantalisingly like the Christian concept of mystical oneness described in *Romans* chapter 12, verse 5: "So we being many are one body in Christ, and every one members one of another".[7] To those of us living in a more secular, digital age it sounds exactly like the worldwide web.

While *Understanding Media* caused a stir in the confines of the academic world and got McLuhan a toehold on the corporate lecture circuit, it was hardly challenging for a top spot on the *New York Times's* list of bestselling books. Or rather it wasn't until Howard Gossage chanced upon it.

McLuhan, do you want to be famous?

As we saw at the end of the last chapter, Gossage felt that "McLuhan's most powerful appeal, in the end, is to those who have thought themselves into a sort of intellectual isolation, who lie awake and groan 'doesn't anyone else think like me?'"

According to his wife, Sally, Gossage was actually lying in bed late one night in February 1965 when his intellectual isolation came abruptly to an end. "I remember I was reading some sort of wonderful novel and Howard was reading Marshall McLuhan's book and he said 'I get it, I understand!' and I said 'What?' and he said 'McLuhan is assuming that the reader already knows the background stuff that McLuhan knows so he's writing in shorthand. It needs to be filled in. I'm going to fix it.' And the next thing I know he's on the 'phone and he's got Marshall McLuhan on the 'phone in Canada and he says 'McLuhan, do you want to be famous?'"[7]

Fortunately, another thing the two men shared in common was the propensity

---

*Here we get a double dose of McLuhan's remarkable foresight. Not only was he predicting the "information economy" in which many of us now work. His idea that electronic media would change the way we think was also so far ahead of its time that it is only now being dealt with. Books like Nicholas Carr's *The Shallows: What the internet is doing to our brains* (2010) and John Brockman's *Is the internet changing the way you think?* (2010) are just two examples of the kind of contemporary 'thought leadership' that has finally started to ask the questions McLuhan answered over 50 years ago.

for calling people at any time of day or night. So it's unlikely that McLuhan was put out by the nocturnal interruption.

Either way, Jerry Mander has a similar recollection of their first contact. "Howard Gossage discovered Marshall McLuhan as far as I can see. He launched Marshall McLuhan. He'd read that book and he said 'Mander, look at this. This guy's fantastic. This is the most amazing person, let's call him up.' At that time McLuhan was not a well-known character. His book had just come out, I don't know how Howard got hold of it but he had read it cover to cover in a flash and said, 'This is the best thing on media that's ever been done', and he called him up on the 'phone and his opening line was 'Dr. McLuhan, how would you like to be famous?' And McLuhan laughed and ... didn't really take him seriously but he talked to him and Howard said 'I'm going to have you out here and we're going to have a two day seminar with a lot of important reporters and they're going to write about you – and you'll be famous' – and that's exactly what happened."[9]

By the time the Firehouse seminar took place in August 1965, Gossage had already delivered on his promise. Back in May, Gossage and his partner Dr. Gerald Feigen in their recently formed consultancy, Generalists, Inc., had invested $6,000 and taken the little-known academic to the East Coast. There, in restaurants afford-able only to those on corporate welfare, he was introduced to the nation's leading media owners, newspaper reporters, TV journalists and admen.

Breathing surprisingly easily in the rarefied atmosphere of the corporate élite, the 53 year-old conservative academic in the striped seersucker suit and plastic clip-on bow tie took delight in telling the people who either ran or had found fame and fortune working in the media that, frankly, they really knew nothing about it.

The ad platform - without the ad

One of the media men was journalist Tom Wolfe who was covering McLuhan's tour for a *New York Herald Tribune* series entitled *The new life out there*. "Looking back, I can see that Gossage, but not McLuhan, knew what was going to happen to McLuhan over the next six months. Namely, that this 53 year-old Canadian English teacher, grey as a park pigeon, would suddenly become an international celebrity and the most famous man his country ever produced."[10]

By the time of this gathering in San Francisco, Gossage had already delivered on his promise to make McLuhan famous. Left to right, front: Walter Landor, Howard Gossage and Tom Wolfe. Left to right back: Alice Lowe, Herb Caen, Justin Herman, Dr. Gerald Feigen and Mr. and Mrs. Marshall McLuhan.

It was Gossage's "ad platform technique" but this time he hadn't even bothered with the "ad". The media did the job for him and amplified McLuhan's message to a highly receptive business world. In his article for the *Herald Tribune*, Tom Wolfe tells of McLuhan taking a call from one big corporation who wanted to fly him to their HQ to deliver a series of lectures. When the subject of his fee arose he whispered to Gossage:

'"How much should I charge?'

'What do you usually get for a lecture?' says Gossage.

'Five hundred dollars'

'Tell him a hundred thousand.'

McLuhan looked appalled.

'Oh all right' says Gossage. 'Tell him fifty thousand.'

McLuhan hesitates then turns back to the telephone: 'Fifty thousand'."[11]

It was then the corporation man's turn to be appalled. McLuhan, one senses, took pity and settled for a mere $25,000.

Gossage delighted in McLuhan's good fortune. Not that he saw any of the money himself for, as Dugald Stermer says, "If he promoted, advanced McLuhan, he didn't get anything in return for it, nor would he want anything in return".[12]

So what was in it for Gossage? A *Business Week* profile explained: "There is no visible payment in these adventures. But if they accomplish nothing more, they will, under Gossage's provocative needling, generate ideas."[13]

Playing it fat, dumb and happy

Gossage was taking the kind of conversation he encouraged in the Firehouse and inviting the entire nation to join in. If it was intellectually stimulating for all concerned, then for Gossage it was also a lot of fun. Indeed, he'd set out on the McLuhan tour with no clearer plan than to "play it fat, dumb and happy".[14] And everything was going according to that plan. Especially the "happy" bit.

The two men certainly appear to have enjoyed each other's company, as this excerpt from a letter to Barrows Mussey suggests. One of McLuhan's myriad theories held that no one stutters in a foreign language. Gossage writes: "I told him 'Marshall, you're full of shit. I stutter in French. I stutter in Spanish ....' He said 'Exactly; it is sublimated.' I replied 'Then drunkenness is a foreign language, too, because I swear like a son-of-a-bitch in High Middle Drunkish.'" And then, with a nod in the direction of the lonely little boy of another incarnation, Gossage concluded, "You should have caught my act in Denver when I was a kid."[15]

No one else treated McLuhan with such irreverence. In fact, he was feted and fawned over. For instance, on one occasion he was offered a permanent office in Manhattan plus other inducements by magazines that were competing for his attentions. As often seemed to be the case, in response he asked Gossage what he should do.

As Tom Wolfe reported, "'Take 'em both!' says Gossage. 'You need offices on both sides of town. Suppose you get caught in traffic?' McLuhan looks puzzled but Gossage is already off into his laugh. . . . His eyes light up like Stars of Bethlehem.

The laugh comes in waves, from far back in the throat, like echoes from Lane 27 of a bowling alley, rolling, booming far beyond the immediate situation, on to ...

"... in any case, McLuhan never failed to provoke this laugh."[16]

Marshall McLuhan. Superstar

While Gossage found him hilarious, everyone else was taking McLuhan very seriously. His genius was celebrated by all those media outlets he mildly rebuked and often ridiculed. Canada's own *Maclean's* magazine was an early convert with its July, 1965 headline: "The High Priest of Pop Culture". American *Playboy* showed its appreciation with: "Marshall McLuhan: Mastermind", and London's *Observer* called him "The Electronic Prophet."[17]

McLuhanacy gathered pace until, in 1966, he was the focus of 120 major features in magazines across the US, Canada and the UK. *Newsweek* splashed him on its cover,

I think this is all I have to say at the moment except that I liked your McLuhan airplane analogy. I'll tell you how Gutenberg McLuhan is.* If (according to ▓▓▓▓ Gerry Feigen) he was sitting on the can constipated for two hours and there was nothing in the place to read except one of his books he'd look at the wallpaper.

Yours.

Gossage

* He admits to being one. I really doubt that he'd have the patience to read or even listen to himself if he wasn't hooked in already. I think him very valuable if one knows enough to screen out the trial balloons; god knows it's work. But I find he holds up. 9 Months now.

Gossage had an irreverent respect for McLuhan, as can be seen from this extract of a letter dated 3 September, 1965 – nine months after his initial contact with the Canadian professor.

and *Life* magazine announced the coming of "the oracle of the electric age".[18] All seemed convinced that here was the thinker whose importance and influence would rival that of Freud.

McLuhan had become, to quote his biographer Douglas Coupland, "A superstar." As Coupland continues, "At a certain point in the mid-1960s he stopped being merely a brainy academic from Toronto. He became a massive brand, as famous and synthetic and misunderstood and misquoted as fellow 1960s media construct and artist Andy Warhol . . . . He was everywhere. He was hip and cool and groovy and far out. He was a fraud, a monster, a genius, and a hoax. Young people loved him. Talk shows were incomplete without him."[19]

No wonder he was so popular in the USA. With his vast knowledge and great gift for pattern recognition here, at last, was an intellectual from the Western Hemisphere who had his own "unified theory of everything". Before McLuhan, the big idea that explained pretty much all aspects of human behaviour had been the preserve of Europeans with Freud, Marx and Darwin the most recent of a line going back to Aristotle and Plato.

To be fair, the Far East had also had its share of thinkers who could put together a half-decent unified field theory. And back at the Firehouse, Alice Lowe, who was of Chinese descent, and a graduate of the ferociously intellectual Reed College in Portland, was certainly less than impressed by the Canadian. "McLuhan was pretty hard to understand because he goes round and round and round. Howard would say 'you mean . . .' and turn it into something an ordinary person could understand. On the wall at the Firehouse there was a lot of graffiti and I think it was Marshall McLuhan that had written 'the Medium is the Message'. Some disrespectful person had crossed out the 'M' and put a 'T'."[20]

What Marshall means is . . .

McLuhan could live with such criticism. Never one to pander to an audience or make an intellectual compromise, he remained defiantly obscure and demanded that his audience try to keep up and think harder. Gossage was doing just that because he was genuinely impressed by the man. As he said, "The difference between McLuhan and me is that by temperament – and experience too – I am the sort who says the

Wright Brothers will never get it off the ground. He is the one who says that every family in America will be flying a private plane by 1950."[21]

If he didn't have McLuhan's visionary optimism, he did share many of his views. As he confided to his friend Barrows Mussey, "McLuhan confirms so many of my elaborate notions."[22] Which explains why, time and again, Gossage was able to point out the brilliance of the new guru's more arcane theories. Occasionally the professor himself seemed to benefit from the explanation. As one witness, Gossage's long-time collaborator, Stan Freberg, recalled, "Gossage had happened on Marshall McLuhan's brilliant but scholarly textbook, *Understanding Media,* and some sort of lightning bolt crashed in his brain. McLuhan would later say that Howard was one of the first people to understand the point of his book. As soon as Howard figured it out, he explained to McLuhan what he, McLuhan, was trying to say."[23]

To clarify things further, Gossage wrote a feature article in *Ramparts* magazine titled "Understanding Marshall McLuhan". In a preface to the article, the *Ramparts* editor Warren Hinckle noted that McLuhan "once remarked that Gossage understood McLuhan better than McLuhan understood McLuhan." That preface also noted how *Understanding Media* had "assumed the crest of the undergraduate popularity wave that once carried J.D. Salinger and then Ayn Rand."[24]

Ramparts's editor Warren Hinckle was, in fact, a very close friend of Gossage and, as such, an eyewitness to McLuhan's reliance upon the adman. He later described their relationship: "Gossage was always kind of translating for the potty prophet: 'What Marshall means by all this is that. . . .' But a lot was added in the translation and McLuhan would look at Gossage like the Mad Hatter peering over the tea cup and say, in a voice that was part confused innocence, part modest genius, 'Gee, Howard, that's exactly what I meant when I wasn't saying it'."[25]

The counterculture's favourite tweed-suited fiftysomething

Whatever it was that McLuhan wasn't saying, the public lapped it up, and by the late 'sixties millions shared Gossage's enthusiasm. Foremost amongst these were the hippies and members of the counterculture who were gravitating toward San Francisco. James Harkin explains the connection, "For McLuhan, the birth of this new electronic medium held out the prospect of pooling our human consciousness in a single global brain or global village .... The key tenet of the counterculture's intellectual heavyweights was that everything on earth was tied to everything else in an organic whole ....."[26]

That was certainly the opinion of the hippies' intellectual heavyweight champ, Stewart Brand. In Chapter 7, we'll see that Brand was himself no stranger to the Firehouse and that he went there to plan an event that was to shape the development of the counterculture (and the rock industry, too).

While there's no record of him meeting McLuhan at Gossage's agency, he was certainly influenced by the man. Moreover, like other key players in this story, he also took Norbert Wiener's theories as his inspiration. As James Harkin writes, "Both McLuhan and Brand had been deeply and formatively influenced by the cybernetics of Norbert Wiener and his ideas about how humans could benefit from being tied together in a continuous information loop of instruction and feedback."[27]

For Brand and the other members of the counterculture, there was a huge benefit in such continuous but closed loops: they were beyond the Establishment's control. Not only that, when those hippies headed off to the desert to escape the authoritarian representatives of the Military-Industrial Complex, their feedback loops allowed for the kind of connectivity and self-regulation that enabled their communes to function.

Typically, Stewart Brand was the first to apply Wiener and McLuhan's principles on a grand scale with something he called the *Whole Earth Catalog*. This was the Wiener instruction/feedback loop in paper form i.e. a huge brochure comprising a melange of unrelated news items, features and general musings.*

Wiki in paperback form

Aimed at a hippie audience trying to forge a life outside mainstream society, there were advertisements for buckskin, beads and books. More specifically, there was an

---

*If Stewart Brand learned his cybernetic theory from Wiener and McLuhan, then he was also greatly influenced by another cybernetic guru who gravitated to the Firehouse. Buckminster Fuller, the early advocate of solar energy, wind power and sustainability, was a regular attendee of the Firehouse lunches and an enthusiastic member of Gossage's intellectual inner circle. Incidentally, the Firehouse connection with the Whole Earth Catalog doesn't end there. Brand's friend, Jerry Mander, also sat on its board.

ad for Norbert Wiener's *Cybernetics — or Control and Communication in the Animal and the Machine* — \$1.95 postpaid. This came complete with a laudatory review which began "McLuhan's assertion that computers constitute an extension of the human nervous system is an accurate historical statement" and concluded with "Norbert Wiener has the story, and to some extent, is the story".

Hippie readers were encouraged to not merely purchase but to participate directly by embellishing the *Catalog* with their own observations, suggestions, advertisements and ideas until what emerged was a publication that seemed somehow to be printing and producing itself.

In years to come the *Whole Earth Catalog* was described by Apple founder Steve Jobs as "sort of like Google in paperback form, 35 years before Google came along."[28] In fact, it seems more appropriate to say Brand introduced his rudimentary wiki a good 25 years before Ward Cunningham created his WikiWikiWeb and 40 years before anyone else started talking about open sourcing, crowd sourcing or other such collaborative ways of working.

From 1967 to 1971, the *Catalog* was required reading for the half a million Americans who moved out of the cities and back to the land. It was one of the biggest and fastest mass migrations in American history. Unlike others, however, it wasn't propelled by want and economic hardship. On the contrary; for many it was a by-product of plenty, and when the post-war economic boom that made such rebellion possible finally stalled, the various hippie tribes folded up their teepees and went back to their air conditioned reservations.

Undeterred, Brand and other Bay Area veterans of the counterculture set about making McLuhan's prophecies real. And they did so not by projecting them onto TV screens, as McLuhan predicted, but by plugging them into a network of "personal computers" — a term, incidentally, that first appeared in Brand's 1974 book, *II Cybernetic Frontiers*.

While Brand and the electro-hippies experimented with ever more effective ways of creating such a network, their old mentor, McLuhan faded from public view. As the most astute observer of the impact of modern media on man, he'd have seen the irony in becoming what Daniel J. Boorstin saw as the inevitable and ephemeral product of the pseudo-event: "The celebrity ... a person who is well known for his well-knownness."[29]

As *HotWired*'s Gary Wolf was later to explain, he'd "chopped up his promising scholarly career into hundreds of thousands of jokes, quips, bad puns, inane television commentaries, and letters to the editor."[30] When those television shows and editors moved on to the next big thing, McLuhan's jealous academic detractors moved in for the kill. And he died in 1980, ridiculed, stroke-ridden and, cruellest of all for such a brilliant and garrulous man, unable to speak.

We're all his cybernetic creatures now

McLuhan never lived to see Stewart Brand create his community-based network in 1985. He called it the Whole Earth 'Lectronic Link or the WELL, and from its name alone we can see this was the hi-tech version of the *Catalog* – his print-based experiment in cybernetics.

The WELL wasn't the internet, but the people who helped Brand create it – the hackers, hobbyists, engineers, programmers, journalists, musicians and academics – were to apply their shared experience to become the net's most influential innovators.

Moreover, they remembered to pay their debt to the most innovative thinker of the electronic age. In 1993 a former editor of Brand's *Whole Earth Catalog*, Kevin Kelly, launched a magazine called *Wired* which immediately pronounced McLuhan the "Patron Saint of the Digital Age".

Paying homage to their saint were the individuals who were to set the philosophical agenda for the development of the worldwide web. As James Harkin explains, "By the early 'nineties many of the prime movers and best thinkers in the electro-hippie movement were congregating around *Wired* which, as we know, was to play a hugely influential role in the development of the internet. People like Kelly, Nicholas Negroponte and others were saying that McLuhan had been its early prophet and that they were now his apostles there to announce that his prophecies were correct and that this second coming had, in fact, arrived and was all around us in the global electronic network."[31]

Bringing McLuhan's prophecies right up to date, Harkin is in no doubt about his status as "the most significant internet thinker ... and an incredibly prescient prophet. Here we are 50 years after he wrote much of his work and it turns out, in fact, that many of us spend much of our time in places like Facebook, on Twitter, on blogs constantly sending out information and learning to rapidly respond to feedback, until we've become the cybernetic creatures that he wanted us to become."[32]

Fittingly, the last word should go to Tom Wolfe, whose writings in the mid-'sixties did so much to make McLuhan famous: "He never lived to see the computer develop into a communications medium (and) no doubt the internet would have delighted him. He would have seen it as a fulfilment of prophecies he made 30 years before it was born, as a more direct, intimately tribal form of the global village than television – and as an even more likely instrument for the realisation of his dream of a mystical unity of all mankind."[33]

Facebook circa 1965

Howard Gossage didn't live to see the computer develop into a communications medium either. More pertinently, the father of interactive advertising never got the chance to harness its capabilities. But, as with McLuhan, the more astute digital natives have come to acknowledge his legacy.

One of the most successful of them, Alex Bogusky, describes Gossage as "a huge hero of mine".[34]

Bogusky was creative director at the advertising agency Crispin Porter when he fell under Gossage's spell in the early 'nineties. As he recalls, "The ads were different from anything I'd seen in that they seemed to live at a level just above advertising. They were conversations with an audience and often designed to let the audience speak back. This seemed like a high-wire act compared to most advertising. It had a certain virtuosity to it. And I aspired to do the same. While we lacked his talent, we had a big advantage that Gossage didn't. The newly minted worldwide web, as we called it back then."[35]

Then again, Gossage seemed to be doing OK with print ads and coupons. In fact, it wasn't just his unique style of interactive advertising that anticipated the internet by 40 years, he also got to a rudimentary form of social media twenty years before Mark Zuckerberg's parents were even friends.

As Professor Greg Pabst, Program Director, Advertising, at the University of San Francisco says, "Howard put together organic communities, he let people want to opt in. He understood that we all want to belong to something, some kind of club."[36]

As Gossage himself observed in an internal memo to his colleagues in 1959, "Let the audience in on the gag. Better still, let them know that you know that they know; this makes it cozier and much more involving. You see, the objective is not fun and games but warmth and community of interest."[37]

According to Professor Pabst, that "community of interest" can be seen in all those people who drove around with Fina's pink valve cap fitted to their car; followed John F. Stahl's walk to Seattle; wore their Beethoven Sweatshirts or, being avid Mozart fans, formed their own sub-community "The Wolfgang Club"; the thousands who wrote in to Eagle Shirts with their suggestions on a use for the shirtkerchief or a new colour to describe the range; and the amateur aerospace engineers who entered wholeheartedly into the madness of the paper airplane competition. All of them, clipping the coupons and playing their part, were finding togetherness and a shared sensibility.

As Professor Pabst concludes, "It all worked because everyone felt like they were a part of a family, they were part of a community. He didn't have Facebook to do it. He did it with ink and paper – and it worked."[38]

Creating *The New Yorker* community

Gossage actually used the terminology of social media to describe his audience. As his wife Sally observes, "He regarded them as his 'friends'."[39] This certainly supports the view of contemporary advertising chief Jeff Goodby that, "He always felt the people who read his ads were his friends ... I think he hoped he was a beacon to the people who read his ads and that they would somehow feel like they knew him just by taking part in these things. He was friending people long before anybody friended anything .... It's like a Facebook page, it's like communicating to the world through *The New Yorker* as your Facebook Page."[40]

As Goodby suggests, whereas today we find out what our friends are doing by logging on to Facebook, these individuals kept abreast of theirs by opening the pages of *The New Yorker* magazine. As Marshall McLuhan would have it, to the reader, *The*

New Yorker was both an extension of the individual and a place of communion to which they came for their shared experience.

Professor Fred Turner sees the parallel, but traces it back to its original inspiration, "The part of McLuhan that might have enabled Gossage to build communities, I would argue, came from his reading of Norbert Wiener, and the idea that communities could be built through the exchange of information."[41]

Professor Pabst agrees: "Howard read Norbert Wiener and *Cybernetics* and he'd be so excited if he were here today with Facebook which gives you instant feedback. He would have been telling us about it, he would have been writing about it and he would be changing the world just as he did 50 years ago".[42]

The epitaph he dreaded

At the time he was launching Marshall McLuhan on the path to digital sainthood, Gossage's preoccupations were not yet global.

But his interest in McLuhan and his decision to get the conversation started with a national audience can be seen as an expression of a broadening outlook. Alice Lowe certainly thinks so. As she says, "What did Howard gain from helping McLuhan? The knowledge that he was helping others … helping Marshall McLuhan made him feel that he was doing good."[43]

And it could be that his experience of working with the visionary McLuhan opened his eyes to an even bigger picture. Until then, his role as adman had confined him to a narrow commercial canvas. Admittedly, his unique style of advertising was more humane, more democratic. He had also found a way of building communities in what was an ever more impersonal and alienating world.

But increasingly, building those commercial communities wasn't enough for him. As he complained to his wife Sally, "I'll have done nothing that means anything to anyone in this world except maybe invented the Beethoven sweatshirt" and, as Sally realised, that was an epitaph he dreaded.[44]

Jerry Mander explains Gossage's frustration this way, "He got to the edge of dealing with serious questions about society [and] I think he had a social/political/justice right and wrong meter inside him all along, and was sensitive to it. He just hadn't found a way of expressing it in his advertising."[45]

That opportunity came in the year after the McLuhan adventure. And when it arrived, Gossage was able to use his interactive style to help start a community that would ultimately become so vast and influential that it remains one of the most important social, political and economic phenomena of the late 20th and early 21st centuries.

Chapter 6

SAVING
THE GRAND CANYON
AND STARTING
THE GREEN MOVEMENT

"DON'T PUT RAISINS IN THE MATZOHS"

When David Brower called at the Firehouse in May, 1966 he wasn't there to get Howard Gossage to work on his advertising. He reckoned he could do a better ad himself. In fact, he'd just written it. All he wanted was for Marget Larsen to do the design and lay it out.

The advertisement was about the imminent threat to dam and, in so doing, desecrate the USA's most visually breathtaking and geologically important national monument, the Grand Canyon.

Brower came to the Firehouse as the executive director of the Sierra Club, a non-profit organisation dedicated to the enjoyment and preservation of America's natural habitat. At the time it had about 35,000 members for whom it organised trips into the wild, produced films and published handsome *Exhibit Format Series* books of stunning landscape photography.

In addition, for years the Sierra Club had fought to protect the American wilderness and had achieved many successes — most notably the protracted campaign that prevented the building of the Echo Park dam in the middle of Dinosaur National Monument in 1956.

David Brower had dedicated his life to such causes. It was he who'd led the battle to preserve Dinosaur National Monument. Other confrontations followed, and Brower increasingly saw the club's role as less an organiser of film shows and excursions, and more the militant vanguard of the budding conservationist movement.

To Brower, protecting the natural habitat was tantamount to a religion, but for most of his early life he'd been a voice crying in the wilderness. As his son, the environmentalist writer Kenneth recalls, "This is a measure of how things changed; when I was at elementary school, people would ask me what my father did and I'd say 'Conservationist' and kids would say, 'What's that?'"[1]

David Brower made it his mission to overcome such ignorance and indifference and, through near obsessive determination, succeeded. Others may have loved the great outdoors as much as Brower, but none were as single-minded or uncompromising in its defence. Kenneth reckons, "It's safe to say that, for the first half of the 20th century, my father was the most influential environmentalist — or conservationist as it was called then."[2]

Usually his campaigns comprised the production of either a Technicolor film or an *Exhibit Format Series* coffee table book, which drew attention to the grandeur of the landscape under threat, followed by political lobbying on a local and national level. But, in May 1966, Brower knew the old tactics weren't working.

Up to their necks in it

He'd already assembled a special task force of technical experts and according to Michael P. Cohen's *The History of the Sierra Club: 1892–1970*, (1988) had then taken the extraordinary step of hiring what Brower called "The MIT Trio: Jeff Ingram, a mathematician who would become Southwest regional representative, Alan Carlin an economist with the Rand Corporation and Lawrence I. Moss a nuclear engineer."[3]

For all the expertise they brought to bear, by the time Brower called in at the Firehouse the plan to dam the Grand Canyon was all but enshrined in law. The bulldozers were already shattering the primordial peace, the scaffolding was up and the drilling had begun. Tom Turner who worked as David Brower's assistant at the Sierra Club recalls that, after over five years of campaigning against it, "the fight was lost. The dams had been approved. They were being supported by the Kennedy Administration much to their shame, I think later, and both Houses of Congress".[4]

They also had the backing of land speculators who knew neither shame nor respect for the law when it came to dealing with opposition. As Martin Litton, a long-time ally of David Brower, recalled, "All those crooks, gangsters and what not were going to be ultra-billionaires from the water that was on their 25 cent an acre land that would suddenly be $25 an acre. A reporter was killed who was investigating the subject from the *Arizona Republic*, the Phoenix paper. His car was blown up, he was blown to bits. That sort of thing was going on. Anyone who dared question the Central Arizona Project was in trouble."[5]

This is pretty damning of the pro-dam faction. The majority, however, were actually a well-meaning group of country boys who were fighting their corner on behalf of the western states and that booming population's need for water. Those who opposed the dams were far removed from the latter day frontiersmen of popular perception. Predominantly they were college-educated, idealists. And fired up college-educated, idealists they were, too. As MIT educated Jeff Ingram recalls, "We were young and full of piss, and we weren't going to let a bunch of water mavens mess up the Grand Canyon."[6]

They may have been "full of piss" but their campaign was in the toilet. Jerry Mander takes up the story: "The Congress had already passed the Bill saying the dams would be part of the Grand Canyon and Stewart Udall, the Secretary of the Interior, was a supporter of them, and it was a done deal. It was all over. Brower was horrified; he'd done everything he could to stop it, and he couldn't. He said, 'We've got to do something different'."[7]

And so, as a desperate last resort, the Sierra Club's beleaguered head wrote his full page "open letter" advertisement and set off to the Firehouse.

What's wrong with charity advertising

Brower was a great admirer of Marget Larsen's art direction and particularly liked the Centaur typeface that featured in many of her layouts. Gossage was, however, reluctant to let her take the job because he knew that, however good the layout, Brower's copy would not get the desired response.

In his opinion, the argument was over elaborate. It was one of Gossage's guiding principles to avoid "putting raisins in the matzohs" i.e. keep things simple, and in this instance he felt Brower was going into too much technical detail.[8]

As a result, Gossage felt that the ad made the same mistake as that of all charity and cause-related advertising: it talked *at* its audience and in so doing alienated the very people who felt most passionately about the cause. By carrying on a monologue in this way it alerted them to the problem without giving them any means of doing something about it. So, rather than embracing the cause, these potential advocates turned against it out of guilt for their own inactivity.

As Gossage explained, "When they [the Sierra Club] came to us for counsel I happened to mention this to them and said, 'What you've got to do is give people recourse. You've got to give them something they can do so they don't feel guilty and, therefore, hate you for making them feel guilty'."[9]

Despite such expert criticism, Brower stood by his "open letter" advertisement. "So", as Jerry Mander recalls, "we agreed to have a competition with him. In those days you could split the run of the paper when you were printing the *New York Times* so that of a two million circulation there's one million of our version and one million of Dave Brower's version. Ours outperformed his enormously."[10]

For the agency's version, Gossage's aim was, as ever, to stimulate feedback. But this time the closed system he was building would expand to allow his readers to get in the loop with those who occupied the highest offices in the land.

The idea was simple: tell the American public about the plans to dam the Colorado River and flood the 140-mile gorge of the Grand Canyon. And tell them it was being done "for profit". Then get them to interact via a series of coupons that ran down the side of the page. Each coupon carried a message to and the return address of, respectively, the President of the United States, the Secretary of the Interior, the Head of the Interior Committee of the House of Representatives, the reader's Congressman, and the reader's two Senators.

Using the internet of the 1960s

While it was Jerry Mander who wrote the copy for that advertisement, he freely admits that the crucial element was the coupons: "Gossage did the important, brilliant thing with those multiple coupons. That had never been done before. They were very, very important because in those days people used coupons; they were their internet. One went to Secretary Udall, one was sent to the president, one was sent to Floyd Dominy who was in charge of the project and they just got a gigantic response. ... Stewart Udall said a few days later that he'd never got so much mail on any subject."[11]

When asked about the coupons, Udall himself thought, "That really was a stroke of genius. Of course, he knew how to put the heat on you. If you were in my position you had to react." [12]

David Brower's son, Kenneth feels there's a lesson still to be learned from Gossage's interactive way of allowing the public to put "the heat on" the people in power. "The coupons in Howard's ads were great in that they did allow people to *do* something. This is a problem with a lot of environmental advocacy which is fine at pointing out the gloom and doom, and getting people angry but not at giving them any place to go. This is what the coupons did and this is how the coupons were enormously effective. It would be nice to apply that Howard lesson to the movement more broadly. We're very good at getting people angry and upset and wanting to do something but not so good at giving them avenues to realise this."[13]

(If they can turn Grand Canyon into a "cash register"
is any national park safe? You know the answer.)

Now Only You Can Save Grand Canyon From Being Flooded…For Profit

Yes, that's right, *Grand Canyon!* The facts are these:

1. Bill H.R. 4671 is now before Rep. Wayne Aspinall's (Colo.) House Committee on Interior and Insular Affairs. This bill provides for two dams—Bridge Canyon and Marble Gorge—which would stop the Colorado River and flood water back into the canyon.

2. Should the bill pass, two standing lakes will fill what is presently 130 miles of canyon gorge. As for the wild, running Colorado River, the canyon's sculptor for 25,000,000 years, it will become dead water.

3. In some places the canyon will be submerged five hundred feet deep. "The most revealing single page of the earth's history," as Joseph Wood Krutch has described the fantastic canyon walls, will be drowned.

The new artificial shoreline will fluctuate on hydroelectric demand. Some days there will only be acres of mud where the flowing river and living canyon now are.

4. Why are these dams being built, then? For commercial power. They are dams of the sort which their sponsor, the Bureau of Reclamation of the Department of the Interior, calls "cash registers."

In other words, these dams aren't even to store water for people and farms, but to provide auxiliary power for industry. Arizona power politics in your Grand Canyon.

Moreover, Arizona doesn't need the dams to carry out its water development. Actually, it would have more water without the dams.

5. For, the most remarkable fact is that, as Congressional hearings have confirmed, seepage and evaporation at these remote damsites would annually *lose* enough water to supply both Phoenix and Tucson.

As for the remainder, far more efficient power sources are available right now, and at lower net cost. For the truth is, that the Grand Canyon dams will cost far more than they can earn.

6. Recognizing the threat to Grand Canyon, the Bureau of the Budget (which speaks for the President on such matters) has already suggested a moratorium on one of the dams and proposed a commission consider alternatives.

This suggestion has been steadily resisted by Mr. Aspinall's House Committee, which continues to proceed with H.R. 4671. It has been actively fought by the Bureau of Reclamation.

7. At the same time, interestingly, other Bureaus within Secretary Udall's domain (notably National Parks, Fish and Wildlife, Indian Affairs, Mines, Outdoor Recreation, Geological Survey) have been discouraged from presenting their findings, obtained at public expense. Only the Reclamation Bureau has been heard.

8. Meanwhile, in a matter of days the bill will be on the floor of Congress and—let us make the shocking fact completely clear—it will probably pass.

The only thing that can stop it is your prompt action.

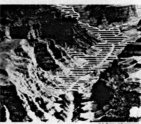

The Grand Canyon : How man plans to improve it. (*Newsweek*, May 30, 1966.)

9. What to do? Letters and wires are effective, and so are the forms at right once you have signed them and mailed them. (You will notice that there is also one in the box below to the Sierra Club; that's us.)

10. Remember, with all the complexities of Washington politics and Arizona politics, and the ins and outs of committees and procedures, there is only one simple, incredible issue here: This time it's the Grand Canyon they want to flood. *The Grand Canyon.*

WHAT THE SIERRA CLUB IS FOR

The Sierra Club, founded in 1892 by John Muir, is nonprofit, supported by people who sense what Thoreau sensed when he wrote, "In wildness is the preservation of the world." The club's program is nationwide, includes wilderness trips, books, and films—and a major effort to protect the remnant of wilderness in the Americas.

There are now twenty chapters, branch offices in New York, Washington, Albuquerque, Seattle, and Los Angeles, and a main office in San Francisco.

This advertisement has been made possible by individual contributions, particularly from our Atlantic, Rocky Mountain, Rio Grande, Southern California and Grand Canyon chapter members, and by buyers of Sierra Club books everywhere, especially the twelve in the highly praised Exhibit Format Series, which includes books on Grand Canyon, Glen Canyon, the Redwoods, the North ern Cascades, Mount Everest, and the Sierra.

Sierra Club
Mills Tower
San Francisco, California

☐ Please send me more of the details of the battle to save Grand Canyon.

☐ I know how much this sort of conservation protest costs. Here is my donation of $_____ to help you continue your work.

☐ Please send me a copy of "Time and the River Flowing" the famous four-color book by Philip Hyde and Francois Leydet which tells the whole story of Grand Canyon and the battle to save it. I am enclosing $25.00.

☐ I would like to be a member of the Sierra Club. Enclosed is $14.00 for entrance fee and first year's dues.

Name
Address
City _____ State _____ Zip _____

Note: All contributions and memberships dues are deductible.

Jerry Mander who wrote the copy for this advertisement says, with typical grace, that the crucial element was the coupons: "Gossage did the important, brilliant thing with those multiple coupons. That had never been done before."

Back in June 1966, the people who were getting angry and upset were suddenly the dam's supporters. For, as Gossage put it at the time, the first advertisement "really made the shit hit the fan."[14] What made it fly was the great emphasis placed upon "the flooding of the gorge". It was a classic example of Gossage saying something that he knew would generate news. And it worked a treat.

On the day the first ad appeared, Congressman Morris Udall who like his brother, Secretary Stewart Udall, was a lifelong liberal and advocate of many environmental causes, rose in the House of Representatives to "express shock and indignation at the dishonest and inflammatory attacks" delivered by the Sierra Club's advertisement.[15]

According to him and the experts he cited (one of whom, incidentally, was David Brower) the damming of the Colorado River would have caused no flooding in the Grand Canyon. Floyd Dominy made the same point, more vehemently, in a later interview: "He [Brower] had the public believing we were going to flood the Grand Canyon National Park from rim to rim. I thought that was very unfair. Sanctimonious, puritan lies – he deliberately lied." [16]

If Congressman Udall and Commissioner Dominy were correct then we should perhaps recall Gossage's view that "reality is not what happens but is controlled by what is written and said about it." And that as well as the revolutionary use of coupons, his advertisement also made use of that tried and tested advertising technique: emotive overstatement.

Either way, the combination was hugely effective, and people power, thus unleashed, quickly prevailed. Especially after the campaign got a helping hand from an unlikely source.

An unexpected gift from the taxman

The day after the first advertisement ran on June 9th, 1966, the Internal Revenue Service sent a letter to the Sierra Club informing them that their long-standing tax-exempt charitable status had been removed. This act of high-powered peevishness turned the volume even higher on the media-amplification that Gossage was aiming at. For, having made front page news across the nation, it suddenly turned a regional issue into a national debate. And overwhelmingly the people were on the side of the Sierra Club. Tom Turner remembers a delighted David Brower saying they "may not

SHOULD WE ALSO FLOOD THE SISTINE CHAPEL SO TOURISTS CAN GET NEARER THE CEILING?

EARTH began four billion years ago and Man two million. The Age of Technology, on the other hand, is hardly a hundred years old, and on our time chart we have been generous to give it even the little line we have.

It seems to us hasty, therefore, during this blip of time, for Man to think of directing his fascinating new tools toward altering irrevocably the forces which made him. Nonetheless, in these few brief years among four billion, wilderness has all but disappeared. And now these:

1) There is a bill in Congress to "improve" Grand Canyon. Two dams will back up artificial lakes into 148 miles of canyon gorge. This will benefit tourists in power boats, it is argued, who will enjoy viewing the canyon wall more closely. (See headline). Submerged underneath the tourists will be part of the most revealing single page of earth's history. The lakes will be as deep as 600 feet (deeper for example, than all but a handful of New York buildings are high) but in a century, silting will have replaced the water with that much mud, wall to wall.

There is no part of the wild Colorado River, the Grand Canyon's sculptor, that will not be maimed.

Tourist recreation, as a reason for the dams, is in fact an afterthought. The Bureau of Reclamation, which backs them, prefers to call the dams "cash registers." They are expected to make money by sale of commercial power.

They will not provide anyone with water.

2) In Northern California, four lumber companies are about to complete logging the private virgin redwood forests, an operation which to give you an idea of its size, has taken fifty years.

Soon, where nature's tallest living things have stood silently since the age of the dinosaurs, the extent of the cutting will make creation of a redwood national park absurd.

The companies have said tourists want only enough roadside trees for the snapping of photos. They offer to spare trees for this purpose, and not much more. The result will remind you of the places on your face you missed while you were shaving.

3) And up the Hudson, there are plans for a power complex — a plant, transmission lines, and a reservoir on top of Storm King Mountain — destroying one of the last wild and high and beautiful spots near New York City.

4) A proposal to flood a region in Alaska as large as Lake Erie would eliminate at once the breeding grounds of more wildlife than conservationists have preserved in history.

5) In San Francisco, real estate developers are day by day filling a bay that made the city famous, putting tract houses over the fill; and now there's a new idea — still more fill, enough for an air cargo terminal as big as Manhattan.

There exists today a mentality which can conceive such destruction, giving commerce as ample reason. For 74 years, the 40,000 member Sierra Club has opposed that mentality. But now, when even Grand Canyon can be threatened, we are at a critical moment in time.

This generation will decide if something untrammelled and free remains, as testimony we had love for those who follow.

We have been taking ads, therefore, asking people to write their Congressmen and Senators; Secretary of the Interior Stewart Udall; The President; and to send us funds to continue the battle. Thousands have written, but meanwhile, the Grand Canyon legislation has advanced out of committee and is at a crucial stage in Congress. More letters are needed and more money, to help fight a mentality that may decide Man no longer needs nature.*

David Brower, Executive Director
Sierra Club
Mills Tower, San Francisco
☐ Please send me more details on how I may help.
☐ Here is a donation of $_____ to continue your effort to keep the public informed.
☐ Send me "Time and the River Flowing," famous four color book which tells the complete story of Grand Canyon, and why T. Roosevelt said, "leave it as it is." ($25.00)
☐ Send me "The Last Redwoods" which tells the complete story of the opportunity as well as the destruction in the redwoods. ($17.50)
☐ I would like to be a member of the Sierra Club. Enclosed is $14.00 for entrance and first year's dues.
Name_____
Address_____
City_____ State_____ Zip_____

*The previous ads, urging that readers exercise a constitutional right of petition, to save Grand Canyon, produced an unprecedented reaction by the Internal Revenue Service threatening our tax deductible status. IRS says the ads may be a "substantial" effort to "influence legislation." Undefined, these terms leave organizations like ours at the mercy of administrative whim. (The question has not been raised with any organizations that favor Grand Canyon dams.) So we cannot now promise that contributions you send us are deductible — pending results of what may be a long legal battle.

The Sierra Club, founded in 1892 by John Muir, is nonprofit, supported by people who, like Thoreau, believe "In wildness is the preservation of the world." The club's program is nationwide, includes wilderness trips, books and films — as well as such efforts as this to protect the remnant of wilderness in the Americas. There are now twenty chapters, branch offices in New York (Biltmore Hotel), Washington (Dupont Circle Building), Los Angeles (Auditorium Building), Albuquerque, Seattle, and main office in San Francisco.

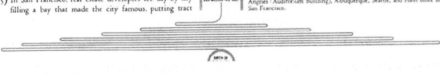

This, and other ads, placed emphasis upon the flooding of 148 miles of the Grand Canyon's gorge — a point which many of the dams' supporters regarded as a scaremongering lie.

know what they think about the Sierra Club, but they certainly know what they think about the IRS."[17]

That support grew ever stronger as more advertisements appeared aimed at stoking the media fire. The most memorable carried the headline, "Should we also flood the Sistine Chapel so tourists can get nearer the ceiling?" With characteristic grace, Jerry Mander concedes, "I didn't write the Sistine Chapel headline. At the Congressional Hearing, Commissioner Floyd Dominy had said tourists would love it. There would be lakes and they would be in their boats right up against the beautiful walls. So Hugh Nash, who was an employee of the Sierra Club, answered back to Dominy, 'Should we also flood the Sistine Chapel so tourist can get a better view of the ceiling?' I read that in the testimony and thought 'Wow!'"[18]

Such was the success of the advertisements and the interest they helped generate that the bill designed to OK the building of the dams never made it to the floor of the House.

It was Stewart Udall who finally made the decision to withdraw in December, 1966 having, in response to the thousands of letters he'd received, taken a trip through the Grand Canyon National Park with his family. As he said, "That was, of course, a victory for the Sierra Club. I think it was a victory for conservation. And I'm proud of the fact that I changed my mind."[19]

A kick-start for environmental activism

It was also a victory for the Gossage agency. Looking back, Jerry Mander is certain that the advertisements played a pivotal role in stopping the dams being built. But more than that, he also sees them as the starting point for what we now know as environmental activism. "Stewart Udall, the Secretary of the Interior, credited those ads with changing the movement and I think many people since have said they changed the character of what was formerly a kind of 'companions on the trail' club to an activist, mainstream organisation with real political clout. It put the environmental movement very much in play."[20]

Kenneth Brower agrees. "The ads focused this campaign, they brought a lot of the activist people in. The people who sat down in the Grand Canyon, held up placards, wrote to their Congressmen; this really was the first time that Americans

David Brower, the father of modern environmentalism, with his supporters in the Grand Canyon. As Jerry Mander says, the ads that rallied that support turned it into "an activist, mainstream organisation with real political clout."

confronted government in this way and I think the ads were crucial. They were not all that was happening but they were certainly at the centre of things."[21]

As he says, "They were not all that was happening". The growing sense of popular unrest had several sources. In 1962 a governmental scientist, Rachel Carson, wrote her bestselling book *Silent Spring* and caused a furore about the use of agricultural pesticides and their carcinogenic effect on man, and their equally lethal impact on wildlife.

Then, under concerted pressure from the Sierra Club and its long-time ally The Wilderness Society, the government passed enlightened acts aimed at preservation and conservation. The most important being The Wilderness Act of 1964 which made the USA the first country in the world to introduce a law that designated vast tracts as permanent wilderness.

In May of the following year, President Lyndon Johnson, whose wife Lady Bird was becoming a very active advocate of conservation, called "The White House Conference on Natural Beauty". We get a sense of the Johnson Administration's growing unease from the president's introductory notes: "The modern technology that has added much to our lives can also have a darker side. Its uncontrolled waste products are menacing the world we live in, our enjoyment, our health. The air we breathe, our water, our soil and wildlife, are being blighted by the poisons and chemicals which are the byproducts of technology and industry."[22]

Earth Day, 1970. And beyond

If the Grand Canyon campaign was not the only stimulus for the Green Movement in the United States, those close to the action in 1966 are sure of its significance in building a shared consciousness, a sense of belonging, and Gossage's great gift to his participating readers: a feeling of community.

According to most observers, that community first found its national voice and a media presence when 20 million people across the USA rallied on Earth Day, 21 March, 1970. Tom Turner, who has been highly active in the Green Movement since those days, believes, "The Sierra Club's activities were a key to the lead up to Earth Day. They weren't the whole thing by any means, there were things happening all over the country but the Sierra Club in particular and the ads for the Grand Canyon were a big spark. They catapulted the concern quite a bit higher than it had been before. It was a stimulus and a catalyst for all that came later. This episode, and the Gossage agency, played an important part in it and not enough people know that."[23]

Kenneth Brower goes even further. In Gossage's interactive advertising, he sees the roots of the more aggressive activism that was to come: "You can draw a line between the coupon in the Gossage ads which allowed people to do something and a more radical environmentalism than my father's. My father, radical as he was, worked within the system and believed that's where it had to be solved. But very shortly after that there came people who took the basic coupon lesson and really ran away with it. People like Dave Foreman who were advocating blowing up transmission towers and logging equipment."[24]

Moving to the present day, one of America's most prominent environmental activists certainly sees the importance in Gossage's "interactive" approach. Julia Butterfly Hill, who from 10 December, 1997 spent 738 days in the branches of an endangered 1,500 year old California redwood tree, believes that "the ads not only provided information and inspiration but they took concepts that would otherwise be overwhelming and flipped them in such a way that they grabbed your attention. That is vital, taking a world view and tweaking it just enough to see it in a new way so we can move forward."[25]

A new style of advocacy advertising

If the Grand Canyon advertising campaign had a big influence on the development of what was to become North America's Green Movement, then it also had an immediate impact upon both the Gossage agency and the Sierra Club.

As we'll see in the next chapter, the agency became famous for its cause-related work. Indeed, it's true to say that it developed what we today describe as "social marketing". According to Jerry Mander who wrote most of those advertisements, "We had gained public attention for having invented a new style of advocacy advertising.... The ads had not only affected policy, they catalysed and organised the public, because they allowed a new level of involvement. By mailing back, people became more committed to the issue. For once they were doing something more than feeling bad."[26]

It's worth noting that there's little evidence in any of these advertisements of the "parallel structures" that characterised Gossage' earlier work. There was no wandering off for a seemingly unrelated conversation before bringing the reader back to the problem that needed solving at the end of the advertisement. "Should we also flood the Sistine Chapel so tourists can get nearer the ceiling" and "Now only you can save Grand Canyon from being flooded ... for profit" were as direct and to the point about the problem that needed solving as any conventional ad could be.

As we've seen, the direct approach was remarkably effective. And such success spurred Gossage on to, once more, berate his advertising peers. As victory in the Grand Canyon beckoned, he told one audience that "all the courageous statements made by the advertising industry could be inscribed on a 5 milligram Benzedrine tablet."[27]

Gossage would also have said that it wasn't just the ad industry that lacked courage. The people on the Sierra Club board were unnerved by the ads that Brower and his agency were producing. And despite, and more accurately because of, the success of the Grand Canyon campaign, they wanted their executive director out.

Offending one president. Insulting another

For Brower's colleagues on the Sierra Club's board, the price paid for that success was too high. First in terms of the club's reputation, and then in money.

Reputation-wise, the advertisements were considered offensive because of what many thought were the gross exaggerations and misleading claims they made about the flooding of the Canyon, and the heat they put upon the people responsible for either promoting the dams or deciding their future.

The Sierra Club's president, Richard Leonard who'd originally fought for Brower to become executive director in 1952 and stood alongside him throughout the Dinosaur National Monument battle, felt those ads were insulting to President Johnson and Stewart Udall. He was not alone in his opposition. Other life-long, committed conservationists had had enough. In April 1967, seven past presidents of the Sierra Club wrote a letter criticizing "the biased, emotional, and irresponsible statements" being put out by "the executive director and his sympathisers."[28]

Money-wise, the rot set in when the first of the Grand Canyon ads caused the Sierra Club to lose its tax-free charitable status. While some members felt the loss of revenue was compensated for by the freedom to play a more confrontational role, others, who wanted to embrace nature and eschew politics, said the money would be sorely missed.

In truth, Brower was never good at balancing the budget and had already run up sizeable losses that threatened to escalate when he began paying for full page advertisements in the *New York Times* and the *Washington Post*.

While many people liked those advertisements, some Sierra Club members saw them as an unnecessary additional expense. And when they caused the loss of the tax-exemption, they seemed even more like a profligate, bad idea.

For a while, the success of the Grand Canyon campaign and other high profile wins protected Brower from his critics. But confrontation couldn't be avoided. And, once again, it was an advertisement from the Gossage agency that brought the issue to a head.

Earth National Park

You could say that the ad in question did actually come out of Madison Avenue, for it began life over a long night's drinking at the New York Biltmore Hotel which once graced an entire block on "Ulcer Gulch". Brower was there with Gossage and Mander and the conversation turned to the controversial new book, *The Population Bomb* (1968) which the authors, Paul and Anne Ehrlich, had been encouraged to write by Brower himself.

Its original intended title, *Population, Resources and Environment* gives a more accurate picture of its concerns about the exploitation and exhaustion of the world's resources. As we'll see in the next chapter's telling of the Anguilla adventure, Gossage had his own solution for such problems. David Brower did, too. He reckoned that, instead of parochial attempts to save national parks and areas of natural beauty, those who cared should be regarding the whole earth as a conservation district.*

With that as their brief, Gossage and Mander created a full page advertisement with the headline: "Earth National Park" and over 1500 words (excluding the coupon copy) that railed against everything from deforestation and pesticides to the building of dams in Egypt, Alaska, Brazil and Laos. The Sierra Club had clearly gone international at a time when no one was thinking in terms of the global effect of man's impact on the natural world.

As with the Grand Canyon campaign, the advertisement carried a call to action aimed at getting people to send a coupon to the president (in this case Richard Nixon) and contacting their congressman. The ad also carried a coupon enabling readers to make a donation to the Sierra Club, and another allowing them to take out membership and order one of a dozen *Exhibit Format Books*.

Those last fundraising coupons were, in fact, an attempt by Brower to hang on to his job. For, in full knowledge that such a radical advertisement would never get approved by his board, he had gone ahead and run it without asking their permission. Which meant that the first time most of the board became aware of

---

*According to his son, Kenneth, David Brower had come "to see the earth as a living system." [29] If so, then he was sharing the same cybernetic vision as his half-brothers in the ecology movement. They, too, had started to see the world in terms of closed systems. Indeed, they coined the term 'ecosystem' and built round it the (now discredited) idea of a self-regulating natural world existing in harmoniously balanced order.

the Sierra Club's emergence on the world stage of environmental activism was when they opened their copies of the *New York Times*.

Those who had already parted ideological company with Brower were furious, and few were appeased when he excused himself by saying that the ad was being paid for out of his publications budget, and that the promotion for the *Exhibit Format Books* would cover the cost.

From then on, Brower had as much chance of survival as a potted plant at a loggers' convention.

Leaving the Sierra Club …

The end came when the Pacific Gas+Electric Company proposed building a nuclear plant at Nipomo Dunes on the south-central coast of California. The Sierra Club fought this not because they were against nuclear power, but because Nipomo Dunes was so beautiful. The board promised PG+E that if it spared the dunes by shifting the plant to a new site at Diablo Canyon then there would be no opposition to its construction. Brower saw this as a sell-out, refused to compromise and was forced to resign.

At that point, the newly emerging muscular environmental movement could have returned to being, in the words of Jerry Mander, "the province of bird watchers and little old ladies in tennis shoes."[30]

However, after the press conference announcing his departure, he hinted at a new venture. "I haven't given up the fight but I've moved out of the Sierra Club, not out as a member, but into another sphere of activity that I hope will augment what the Sierra Club is doing and will carry on things that the Sierra Club is not willing or able to do. It's an organisation we don't have a name for yet but I think we'll have an announcement about it by the end of the week."[31]

Brower didn't have to wait that long because the problem of the name was solved when, straight after that interview on 4 May, 1969, Brower called in to the Gossage agency to break the news about his resignation.

As Gossage's wife Sally recalls: "I was at the Firehouse standing next to Howard when David Brower came up and said he was leaving the Sierra Club, which was a shock to me. He said he was going to form his own organisation and he needed a name for it." Gossage was very much aware of Brower's interest in extending the global reach of the environmental movement. According to Sally, he thought about it for a few seconds and said, "Why don't you call it 'Friends of the Earth?'"[32]*

... and moving into the Firehouse

If, as Sally Kemp says, Gossage gave Brower's new organisation a name, then he also gave it a home.

Jerry Mander who was also there at the Firehouse explains, "Howard immediately said, 'Just move in. Bring your people and we'll set you up downstairs'. He loaned him furniture and he was off and running ... I don't think he charged him rent, but Alice Lowe would know."[34]

And Alice does know: "I don't think he paid rent. I don't remember; but if he had paid rent, I would!"[35]

Kenneth Brower knew how much his father valued Gossage's help and says, "It was a wonderful thing for Howard to do".[36] His father's enjoyment of Gossage's hospitality didn't stop there for, even before the move, they'd regularly taken long lunches together at the adman's favourite local restaurant, Enrico's on Broadway.

Back at work, Gossage was more than delighted to have his agency create the advertisements that launched Friends of the Earth, and helped them quickly outgrow their two rooms in the Firehouse. As Kenneth Brower recalls, his father "bitterly regretted moving because it wasn't just professionally that Howard meant a lot to him, my father liked Howard's elegance. Anyway, Friends of the Earth moved three streets and then again. And went from that little two or three rooms under Howard's office to 55 sister organisations around the world."[37]

Gossage had, in fact, helped create what is today the world's largest grassroots environmental network with 5,000 local activist groups and over 2,000,000 members and associates. Moreover, his advertisements had helped kick-start a Green Movement that now numbers its supporters in tens of millions. And he did it by producing ads that were controversial, hard-hitting and, to use a word that no one but he was using back then, interactive.

*As with most creation myths, there is more than one version here. Tom Turner, who was working as closely with Brower as anyone at that time, recalls Friends of the Earth being named in his living room in May or June 1969. While Brower is said to have identified his wife Anne as the wordsmith on that occasion, Tom says that Anne always cited him as the one who came up with the name.[33]

Those advertisements, with their use of the 1960s internet, the coupon, their reliance on rudimentary feedback loops and their ability to generate massive publicity once again show how Gossage anticipated communication techniques that would only be adopted forty years later. But, importantly, on this occasion they were being used to achieve something more than a northerly twitch on what Gossage always called "the old sales curve".

With the saving of the Grand Canyon, Gossage was seeing how the building of a broader community with a shared sensibility could serve a higher purpose.

In the process, he'd also encountered and befriended a man who'd dedicated his life to that higher purpose. This exposure to Brower must have had an effect. Gossage had similar charisma but not the noble cause that it could serve. Add the two together in Brower's person and, as far as his fellow countrymen were concerned, what emerged from the victorious Grand Canyon campaign was a true American hero.

Anyone working alongside Brower couldn't help but be inspired. Here's how long-term fellow activist Martin Litton assessed him, "Dave took the bull by the horns and made things right. He didn't just worry, he didn't just aspire to a better world. He helped to make it better and without him, who knows how bad things would be now. He was only one person, he couldn't do everything, but everything he pitched in on made the earth better . . . ."[38]

For a quixotic character like Gossage, the idea of tilting at real giants as Brower did, rather than the windmills on Madison Avenue, must have seemed most appealing. As this idea took hold, his passion for addressing the shortcomings of the advertising industry, and his interests in his commercial clients, faded still further.

Kenneth Brower was a witness to this: "By the time my father and Howard got together, Howard was obviously having his problems being in advertising. They were both in agreement about advertising, they both didn't like it. Howard probably disliked it more than my father."[39]

Increasingly, Gossage's actions reflected this. In the spring of 1967, just a few months after the Grand Canyon campaign was won, a book of his speeches was published in Germany. Its first chapter was headed, "Is advertising worth saving?" As we're about to see, it seems that its author already knew the answer.[40]

His feelings about saving the world, however, were something else entirely.

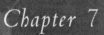

Chapter 7

CHANGING
THE WORLD

"LET'S STIR UP
THE MUSH"

When Howard Gossage set up his agency in 1957, he was convinced that the world needed a better kind of advertising. Ten years later, his view had changed. By then, the only advertising that interested him was that which made for a better kind of world.

His commercial clients no longer excited him. Nor did his old campaign against the boring, bland creative work that had once got him so angry. There's a certain irony in this because, on that front, things were getting better. Indeed, as he lost interest in the fight, the battle over creative style and content suddenly looked winnable.

In February 1966, Rosser Reeves, who had dominated the advertising world when Weiner & Gossage were starting out, shocked the industry by resigning. His departure had been presaged by his agency Ted Bates's loss of the prestigious $8,000,000 Mobil oil account.[1] This was, in itself, a rejection of Reeves's repetitious approach. Insult was added to injury by the fact that the winning agency was Doyle Dane Bernbach.

As we saw earlier, DDB was Gossage's favoured agency when it came to recommending a rival to those clients he either declined to pitch for or wanted to resign. After Gossage did the former to Volkswagen, Bill Bernbach's agency took control of the business and roared off into the distance – with billings worth $27.5 million in 1959 accelerating to $130 million by 1965.[2]

That other creative pioneer, David Ogilvy, experienced similar success in the early 'sixties with the arrival of Shell's $12million annual spend fuelling his growth.[3] However, with his agency attracting ever bigger, more demanding clients, Ogilvy appeared to compromise his principles. As his billings rose, his creative stock fell.

At least, that is, amongst the younger art directors and copywriters who took Bill Bernbach as their hero, and started a wave of new agencies based on his creative principles.

The creative revolution

The first was Papert, Koenig, Lois in 1960; followed, most notably, by Delehanty, Kurnit & Geller in 1961; Carl Ally, Inc. in 1962; Wells, Rich, Greene in 1965; and Della Femina Travisano & Partners a year later.

If Gossage was an iconoclast then the likes of Carl Ally, George Lois and Jerry Della Femina were vandals who took Gossage's intellectual critique of the repetitive approach to advertising and added their own four-letter expletives.

Jeff Goodby pointed up the difference in their styles when he said, "George Lois, the famous art director from New York, said, 'My advertising is like poison gas. I spray it around the room and people fall down'. I think Gossage would have been appalled by that quote. He would have wanted to spray his advertising around and for everyone to feel happy and have a party and all get each other and have senses of humour that seemed to match."[4]

Boorish *enfants terribles* they may have been but the new creative leaders of the "in your face" advertising were merely expressing the spirit of rebellion loose in mid-'sixties America – just as the men in the grey Brooks Brother suits, slim black ties and buzz-cut haircuts had epitomised the conservatism and conformity that characterised the previous decade.

If those organisation men had been happy to work for giant conglomerates like Marion Harper's McCann-Erickson then, in the 'sixties, hundreds of young admen and women left the security and sameness of large agency life to set up their own hotshops.

Free from the controlling influence of the corporate number crunchers, many were willing to apply their skills to radical causes. For example, when George Lois wasn't spreading his "poison gas" he was doing hard-hitting posters for the National Committee for a Sane Nuclear Policy (SANE). From his own pocket he also did the advertising supporting Ruben "Hurricane" Carter, the black boxer wrongfully sentenced to 300 years jail for the murder of three white men.

It was, however, Lois's taboo-busting designs for *Esquire* magazine's front covers that built his radical reputation. For one of those, the *Esquire College Issue* of 1965, Lois chose the four heroes of American youth: Bob Dylan, Malcolm X, Fidel Castro and John F. Kennedy and created a composite face from their features.

At the epicentre of revolt

If that cover resonated with Lois's youthful audience, a part of it would certainly have touched Howard Gossage. As we saw in Chapter 2, Gossage had been a huge Kennedy admirer. Like many Americans, he'd invested his hope in JFK's promise to build a liberal Camelot in 'sixties America. And, like millions of his countrymen, he was devastated when the President died. In Gossage's case, however, the loss stayed with him. As Bob McLaren, the English creative director who he befriended in November 1966 recalls, "Even three years later, the mention of Kennedy's shooting brought tears to his eyes."[5]

Gossage's wife Sally believes that in those three years, the grief served as a catalyst for his own politicisation. If so, then of all his hero's aphorisms, Gossage seemed to take this one to heart: "Every person can make a difference, and every person should try."

This extended far beyond Gossage's previous concern about advertising's short-comings. The shift is understandable when we remember how closely he'd worked with two inspirational men, McLuhan and Brower, who, in their own ways, had dedicated their lives to making the world a better place.

It's also clear that by the mid-'sixties, "stirring up the mush", as he called it, about the ad industry's failings must have seemed trivial.[6] Indeed by then, to get angry about the latest Anacin commercial was to miss the point. America was a nation in flux, and it seemed that its dissenters weren't satisfied with just stirring up the mush. They wanted to kick over the whole bubbling cauldron.

Gossage's own change in perspective must be seen in the context of those turbulent times. As a natural rebel who loved a fight – and, let's not forget, as a self-proclaimed "tediophobe" – the problems of Madison Avenue must have suddenly become just that, tedious. Especially when a real revolution appeared to be raging right there on his doorstep.

There were armed and uniformed Black Panthers patrolling the streets of Oakland just across the Bay; hippies turning Haight-Ashbury into the drug-consuming centre of the western world; and Ken Kesey using the profits from his cult novel *One Flew Over the Cuckoo's Nest* to fund his band of Merry Pranksters as they roamed the San Francisco peninsular propagandising and producing, in massive quantities, the counterculture's drug of choice: LSD.

The Firehouse was also just a 30-minute bus ride from America's most radical university, Berkeley.

Firebrands in the Firehouse

Berkeley's students had launched their attack on the status quo with the Free Speech Movement in 1964. Up until then, university authorities had banned any kind of political activity on campus save that organised by the established Republican and Democratic Party Clubs. When civil rights agitators arrived to recruit new supporters, the authorities called the police and a much-publicised stand-off ensued.

The fight for political and academic freedom became a national cause célèbre. There was more than a little PR in the Free Speech Movement's activities; which is not surprising as Howard Gossage's star copywriter and publicist, Jerry Mander, freely offered his services to its organisers.

And the connection with the Firehouse didn't end there, for the radical students' leader also called in to get Gossage's advice. As Sally Kemp recalls, "The young firebrand Mario Savio of the Free Speech Movement, was leading the riots and the sit-ins at Berkeley, and he came to see Howard at the Firehouse to ask what they needed to do to get themselves heard. He talked to them and was very deeply moved."[7]

It was one of several visits, for the Free Speech Movement had become a client of Generalists, Inc., the consultancy that Gossage ran with Dr. Gerald Feigen. Theirs was an interesting roster for, as Gossage explained in a letter to Barrows Mussey, he and Feigen not only worked with the radical students, "We also had the last chancellor, though the kids nor the U[niversity] know of the other".[8]

He managed to avoid them bumping into each other on the stairs. But only just. As Sally continues, "The very next day, the dean of Berkeley also came to see Howard and asked 'What am I going to do?' Howard listened to him and finally looked at him and said 'If I were you I'd put the school in your wife's name'."[9]

Springtime for the Summer of Love

It wasn't the only time that radical and, in the next case, outlaw elements from the counterculture gathered at the Firehouse. In the winter of 1965, just after Marshall McLuhan had been launched to media stardom, that other soon-to-be hero of the counterculture, Stewart Brand came to see Jerry Mander and asked him to help organise a hippie happening for Ken Kesey's acid-popping Merry Pranksters.

As Mander tells it, "At the time, Kesey was a fugitive and on the run from the police, we needed a safe, secure meeting place so we did it here in the Firehouse with all the doors locked. Kesey was very much a part of the show, but the police were after him."[10]

They certainly were. As mentioned above, for months he'd been leading Brand and his other Merry Pranksters on a very public examination of the consciousness altering properties of LSD; the results of which were written up in Tom Wolfe's *The Electric Kool-Aid Acid Test* (1968). The experiment was over, however, once the Federal government got round to outlawing the drug, and issuing a warrant for Kesey's arrest.

The meeting in the Firehouse passed off uninterrupted. As did the Trips Festival – a three day celebration of the hallucinogenic drug complete with dance, mime, interactive art, movies, light shows, music by the Grateful Dead and, to top it all, a special guest appearance by Marshall McLuhan. Actually the latter, though promised, never happened. Despite that disappointment, the overall impact was massive. As Professor Fred Turner, author of *From Counterculture to Cyberculture*, says, "In January 1966, the Trips Festival was the watershed event for San Francisco and, in effect, America. In its wake we had the Summer of Love where suddenly everyone seemed to have to go to San Francisco with flowers in their hair. It was the moment when tribal San Francisco came into its own. A tribal gathering that would culminate in Woodstock."*[11]

Was Gossage aware of all these things? According to his wife Sally, most certainly: "I don't know if Howard sat in, but he had his ear out for everything that went on."[13] In that case, he must have been amused to know that "the most important event in the San Francisco counterculture", as Fred Turner describes it, was planned in a locked office upstairs in the Firehouse.[14]

---

*When Stewart Brand asked Jerry Mander to help with the Trips Festival, Mander got Bill Graham in to act as the event's promoter. Prior to that, Graham was running the San Francisco Mime Troop but after the success of the Trips Festival (it made $4,000), he came to Mander and asked him if he'd like to partner him in promoting rock concerts at the nearby Fillmore Auditorium, which he was hiring for $50 a week. Jerry thought about it for a few seconds and replied "Nah, I don't think so"; which, he cheerfully admits, is his 'fifth Beatles' moment, as Graham went on from his success at the Fillmore Auditorium to become the biggest promoter in the history of rock music.[12]

Ramparts and radical journalism

We've seen how Jerry Mander has paid tribute to the things that Gossage taught him. However, given his friendship with such leading figures from the counterculture and his commitment to their causes, Jerry Mander must have had an influence on Gossage. Indeed, as Mander and his peers moved leftwards it's easy to see how Gossage, who'd always been a renegade, should himself become ever more radical.

That radicalism found an expression way beyond advertising when Gossage was asked to act as consultant to the Roman Catholic magazine, *Ramparts*. Soon appointed to the board, he encouraged its editor Warren Hinckle to shift leftwards, and to allow his young reporter, Bob Scheer, to stir up as much mush as possible.

It was, for example, *Ramparts* that revealed how the CIA had, for years, been infiltrating and funding the National Student Association. It was in that magazine's pages that black activist Eldridge Cleaver described his elation at seeing Black Panther Huey P. Newton hold a shotgun on a San Francisco policeman right in front of the *Ramparts* office. And it was *Ramparts* that ran its own mini-edition, the *Wall Poster*, chronicling the violence that attended the "police riot" at the Democratic Party Convention in Chicago in 1968.

It wasn't just Hinckle and Scheer's writing that provoked the Establishment. Dugald Stermer, who'd been brought in by Gossage to work on the magazine, produced cover art that made George Lois at *Esquire* look like Norman Rockwell. His work was incendiary and, in the case of the April 1969 edition, insensitive to those whose sons were fighting and dying in Southeast Asia. The cover featured Stermer's own young son holding a Vietcong flag alongside the headline, "Alienation is when your country is at war and you want the other side to win." That cover, and another featuring the staff of *Ramparts* burning their draft cards, caused uproar.

Throughout every controversy, Gossage remained their staunch supporter and their bridge to the power-brokers. As Bob Scheer recalls, "We had the CIA and the FBI swirling all around us, yet the centre of our operations was like an old-fashioned men's club. There'd be Gossage and Herb Caen of the *San Francisco Chronicle* and their friends, and then us wild kids. Those guys would lend us their wisdom, but what was so charming was they never tried to tell us what to do or push us in any direction."

Gossage did, however play an active role on numerous occasions. As Scheer continues, "We survived by getting our story on the front page of the *New York Times* and, if its editor or Sy Hersh got nervous and said 'who the hell are these *Ramparts* guys?', Gossage would step in and reassure them. He did the same thing calming down the magazine's investors when they were getting hysterical – when actually he had nothing to give them, and the investors were right!"[15]

Clearly, through his involvement with *Ramparts*, Howard Gossage wasn't just affected by the turbulence of the times; he was effecting it. This is certainly the view of Peter Richards. He has taken the title of his history of the magazine, *A Bomb in Every Issue* (2009) from a *Time* magazine headline and has subtitled it, *How the Short Unruly Life of Ramparts Magazine Changed America.*

Escaping to Germany

For Gossage, America wasn't changing quickly enough. There were wrongs that needed righting and, in his view, they were much more involving than the problems being brought to him by his commercial clients. Indeed, as his interest in his clients diminished, he started looking for a way out of the day-to-day running of the agency.

One escape route opened up in November 1966 when he was contacted by the Art Directors Club of Germany and invited to make a speech in Frankfurt. It was to be the first of several such excursions.

Whilst there, he became friendly with fellow American writer Barrows Mussey and his wife Dagmar. Mussey was a convert even before the Frankfurt visit for, back in 1964, he'd read an article in *Advertising Age* about Gossage and had persuaded Gossage to send over more of his speeches and writings so they could be amalgamated into a book.

By the time *Ist die Werbung noch zu retten? (Can Advertising be Saved?)* was published in Spring, 1967, Gossage was on his way to becoming a cult. When the Frankfurt office of Young & Rubicam launched Camel cigarettes, mindful of Gossage's Qantas kangaroo, they ran a contest whose first five prizes were camels, delivery of which had to be taken in Beirut. One in ten German adults responded.

Another Y&R copywriter, Walter Luerzer, created a press campaign for Haig

Howard Gossage and Sally with Barrows Mussey on the balcony of their apartment in San Francisco. Mussey and his wife Dagmar helped establish both Gossage's reputation and his business connections in Europe.

Howard Gossage and Sally arriving for dinner on board the SS France. As Sally said, "HLG's dream was to live in a permanent suite on The France, sail around, get off when we wanted to, then catch up with it and keep on".

whisky which was a loving homage to the Firehouse style. Luerzer would remain a Gossage fan for the rest of his professional life which, from 1984 onwards, he dedicated to the furtherance of advertising excellence by publishing *Luerzer's Archive* – the most respected and, when it appears in creative departments every two months, quickly stolen industry publication in the world.

Over in Switzerland, the award-winning GGK agency also adopted Gossage as their consultant, and paid him to visit and lecture to colleagues and clients. For them it was an education; to Gossage it was an escape.

According to Dagmar Mussey who hosted Gossage, his wife Sally and baby daughter Sarah, "Howard enjoyed life so much, and he seemed totally relaxed while he was here. He rarely talked about work, and he never spoke of politics."[16] As his wife Sally explained, "He felt Europeans understood what he was trying to do, and as we both adored travelling, they would pay for us to slip over on *The France* or *Queen Elizabeth* and do business, then romp around from hotel to hotel. HLG's dream was to live in a permanent suite on *The France*, sail around, get off when we wanted to, then catch up with it and keep on. We thought that would be a nice way to end our days."[17]

It was a nice dream, but that First Class lifestyle would take some funding, so Gossage wrote to Barrows Mussey, "I am open to anything: speeches, one night stands, Bar Mitzvahs."[18] At which, the expat began looking for potential clients who might be interested in such services.

Anything but advertising

The most promising was Hubert Burda, the son of one of Germany's biggest magazine publishers. Hubert, who had been an early convert to the Gossage cult, asked Gossage's advice on how he should launch the new men's magazine *M*.

His problem was simple: *M* was to feature a fair degree of bare flesh and Hubert was afraid it would be seen as salacious. All other admen would have recommended a campaign highlighting the magazine's editorial or artistic respectability. Not Gossage. For this was him in his consultant's guise: looking at the world not as a specialist but as the founder of Generalists, Inc.

The aim was to approach each problem with no preconceived idea of what the solution might be. In this case, while advertising was, in fact, the answer, Gossage didn't recommend actually doing any. No, according to him the difference between the respectable and the risqué lay in the advertisements that appeared in a magazine's back pages. If the ads were for aspirational, worthy products and brands then this reflected well on the publication. But if the ads at the back were rude and racy then the reader inferred that the magazine was itself a little louche. In an exercise that would now be a case study in behavioural economics, all Hubert Burda had to do was mediate the experience of the readers who gravitated towards the magazine's back pages. Or as Gossage said, make sure there was "no trashy stuff".[19]

If Gossage was to help Hubert with one of his magazines then the adman hoped the publisher might reciprocate by using the family's expertise and connections to create an international edition of *Ramparts*. Gossage saw a gap in the market for a left-leaning counterpart to the more conservative titles, *Time* and *Newsweek*. Nothing came of that business venture, but the failure didn't blunt their friendship.

Indeed, Burda idolised Gossage, and Gossage had taken to him. So much so that Gossage invited Hubert to join him in New York where he introduced him to a series of leading admen and publishers. He even took him to Chicago to meet the

HOWARD LUCK GOSSAGE

451 PACIFIC, SAN FRANCISCO

11 Jaunary 1968

Dear Mussey,

Thanks for the further rundown. In thinking over the
prurience field and how it has fared I think I see how
Burda could get away with it -- even without the editorial
talent or indignation you speak of. It lies in the use of
contrasts and esdewing the dead giveaways of a naughty
audience. Let's start with that.

The surest way to tell whether a magazine has a raffish
audience-- or xx identity-- is to look at the ads in the back.
If they run to erotica, plain wrapper offerings, depilatories,
etc., then it is simply not respectable, xThix or, let us
say, of the first class. This does not depend on tits or
sexy content, for a Popular Mechanics and the jockstrap
hunting magazines will have a batch of this sort of stuff
too. In any case it gives away a low I.Q. audience. The
difference between Playboy and its imitators -- excluding
treatment editorially-- is in its ads; there is no trashy
stuff there. I notice that Quick is absolutely loaded with
the stuff (more than La Vie Parisienne x in its hey-hey day,
except that LVP didn't hade any general consumer ads and
Quick,in the August issue I have, seems to have quite a
few.) I doubt that the two sorts of ads could coexist in an
American mag; what think you?

So the first thing the new Burda thing ought to do, exclusive
of content is exclude anything in the zippy line, including
falsie and depilatory ads. People are more conscious of this
differentiation than we generally believe-- I believe. Or,
let's say that they are unconscious, but it registers infall-
ibly.

Now, this matter of contrast. Hefner, you will notice,
takes a twist on the old Comstockian variety of titillation
which showed or hinted at everything but cast it all in
depravity by glum faces or predictions of undoubted punishment.
Hefner, on the other hand, makes it all antiseptic but says it
is fun and anyone who thinks this plastic path ends in anything but _real_ primroses is a spoilsport and a pervert of
the sickest sort. Therefore, to accompany his pie-faced
girls (invariably)

No time to finish. See you about the 30th.

Gossage

When Hubert Burda asked Howard Gossage's advice on launching M magazine, the response – as outlined in this letter to Barrows Mussey – was a classic example of Generalist thinking, and an early exercise in what we now know as behavioural economics.

owners of *Advertising Age*. The trip was, as we'll see, to have a lasting impact upon the young man.

Looking for a successor

As the lure of foreign travel became ever stronger, then fortunately in Bob Freeman, Marget Larsen, Dugald Stermer, Alice Lowe, photographer George Dipple and copywriter Richard Stearns, Gossage had a ready, willing and able team back at the Firehouse. Jerry Mander recalls, "He'd just love his staff members to come and take over. He wasn't trying to make a name for himself, he was trying to get out of the business, so the more people wanted to take over, the happier he was."[20]

He went some way to institutionalising their "take over" in 1966 with the launch of Shade Tree, a holding company comprising Intrinsics, the design outfit led by Marget Larsen and Bob Freeman; Generalists, Inc., the consultancy that Gossage ran with Dr. Gerald Feigen; and Freeman & Gossage, the agency that turned out the advertising.

```
                          -5-

I have never really figured out the business-- or the advertising business
in any way I could tolerate-- so that I could perpetuate a system. So I
have settled for dinkiness and making a mild splash every now and again.
If someone came along who could take it over I would let him have it gladly.
But anyone good enough to do that would also have too much ego to allow
him to do it properly, so what the hell.  It worries me, because there
is no prospect at all except the treadmill; which is why I am diversifying.

Oh, one hedge I do have is I will do no point of sale, merchandising,
trade ads, or any of the other things that advertising agencies do.  I
just do ads, and as few of them as I can.  My notion is that it is an
organic thing; you do one ad and see what happens, then you do another.
Unfortunately, this, like other pat systems, breaks down eventually.
Once you have got a client through what I call the propagation stage,
you settle down to turning out a series once a year.  This is something
that someone else can do-- some other nice agency like Doyle, Dane--
as well or even better than I can.  But the hooker is that it is possible
to turn out the occasional block-buster amid all the nice cultivation
ads.  So I allow them to stay on.  Also, I am getting tired.  One
time I asked Jim Young how he happened to get out of advertising, and
he said, "One morning I woke up and I didn't give a damn whether
they sold more Quaker Oats than I did Cream of Wheat".
```

As this letter to Barrows Mussey indicates, by the time of writing (September, 1965) Gossage was already tired of advertising and was looking for a way out.

The President
The White House
Washington 25, D.C.

Mr. President: There is one great forest of redwoods left on earth; but the one you are trying to save isn't it.

...Meanwhile they are cutting down both of them.

THE lumber industry has already cut nearly two million acres of redwoods down to two possible sites for our much-talked-of Redwood National Park.

One of them—Redwood Creek—is magnificent still. The other—Mill Creek ?—Well, it is less unacceptable to the lumber companies.

Soon Congress will decide which of these to save from the saws—which in the meantime buzz on, despite a so-called moratorium on cutting.

It's an old story, Mr. President. In the 1920's there were four great forests left: 1) that along the Eel River and on the Bull Creek and the Dyerville Flats, 2) along the Klamath River, 3) along Redwood Creek, and 4) on the Smith River at Mill Creek.

Considering these as possible sites for *that* year's Redwood National Park, Madison Grant, a founder of the Save-the-Redwoods League, said: "*Each has its peculiar beauty and it is difficult to choose among them.*" And so they didn't.

The lumber companies did, however:

I have just seen the rip-rapped banks of the Eel, and its slash-and-gravel-choked side streams. I saw the high, steep slopes pitifully scarred and eroded by logging. I drove through the great groves left along the Eel—on a high-speed freeway that has effectively and forever ruined the integrity and peaceful beauty of this place.

I walked in the Rockefeller Forest, among the sky-scraping giants, and then saw the glacier of gravel up Bull Creek—the product of catastrophic logging and floods—moving inexorably and lethally toward them.

There is no longer a chance for a great Redwood National Park on the Eel River.

I have just seen the final threats in the destruction of a superlative landscape on the Klamath.

The waters of this river—only a short time ago among the most gorgeous in the northwest—are muddy and roiled and swollen with silt. The high hillsides through which they travel, once clothed in dark, magnificent forests, are now shorn and scraped bare. They are chucking off huge fans of topsoil in a classical display of erosion.

Side streams, long beloved of fishermen, are now gutted and filled with slash—their bright fish gone.

No one talks about a National Park on the Klamath any more.

A few exquisite fragments of the Smith River groves at Mill Creek still remain. They are already protected in California's Jedediah Smith and Del Norte Coast State Parks.

I walked through these in a few hours.

Outside these state parks less than 1,100 acres of superior old-growth redwoods remain in Mill Creek. More than half its forests have been logged.

The proposed park is girdled along the Smith River by summer homes, motels, gas stations and grocery stores. The heart of it has been completely cut out, and now boasts a splendid multi-million dollar industrial complex.

Hardly the stuff a great National Park is made of. Yet Mill Creek would cost us an estimated 60 million dollars.

Much of that would go to buy developed private property. The rest would add only 7,500 acres of virgin redwoods to the existing state parks. (Consider Olympic National Park: nearly 900,000 acres. That, indeed, is preserving the marvelous Douglas Fir forests of Washington for the enjoyment of people for all time. Can we seriously be talking about adding only 7,500 *virgin* acres to our present state parks to preserve the incomparable redwoods? And this for $60,000,000?)

Yet this is the site that the Secretary of the Interior has espoused on behalf of the Administration, because he "wanted to pick a park, not a fight." Not a fight with the lumber industry, anyway.

One last chance remains: Redwood Creek.

In 1920 Madison Grant called it "peculiarly adapted for a national park." In 1964, after fifteen months of study, National Park Service planners called it the finest large block of redwoods left, in terms of park values.

This was confirmed, at one time or another, by conservation groups throughout America. And it was re-confirmed *this year* by the Hammon, Jensen and Wallen report to the Secretary of the Interior.

I was four days exploring Redwood Creek and its drainages this trip. Even then I saw only a fraction of the area I and other Sierra Club members have been looking into for four years. For there are great reaches of it not yet penetrated by logging roads—a unique circumstance in what is left of the redwood country.

The last long stretches of virgin acres in all the redwood region are at Redwood Creek: 20 miles and 14,000 acres of them. And there are more than 10,000 acres of superior old-growth stands. *Ten times what is left at Mill Creek.*

The last virgin forests on both sides of a river are at Redwood Creek; over four miles of them, including the magnificent Emerald Mile.

In short, the last chance to preserve the entire ecological variety of the redwood species—from the ocean shore at Gold Bluffs Beach through inland stands of near rain-forest luxuriance to 3,000 foot high mountain ridges, is at Redwood Creek.

And it is here that the National Geographic Society discovered the tallest tree on earth—and where the second, third, fourth, sixth, eighth, ninth, and tenth tallest trees were subsequently discovered.

Clearly then the $60,000,000 mentioned as the price of a park at Mill Creek would buy far more at Redwood Creek. If indeed $60,000,000—the equivalent of but 2 days' work on federal highway construction projects—is all the money available.

$140,000,000—*but 3 more days of highway building*—would give us the great national park we ought to have.

Meanwhile they are cutting it down. The area the National Park Service recommended for preservation *in 1964*, that named at Senate hearings as the best possible Redwood National Park by 94% of those who favor any park at all; the subject of Senate and House Redwood National Park bills sponsored by 17 Senators* (S. 514) and 41 Congressmen** (H.R. 2849, for example) *is being cut down.*

Mr. President, the Sierra Club and most of its 53,000 members, the 58 Congressmen listed below—and we believe *all* conservationists, were some of them not afraid that lumber interests had ruled it out already—are convinced that Redwood Creek is the only national park this wealthiest nation in history can afford to establish.

Speaking for them, and for future generations with every interest in the creation of the park—but no voice in it—I urge you to reconsider the site of the Administration's proposed Redwood National Park, while there is still time.

Yours sincerely,

Edgar Wayburn, President
Sierra Club, Mills Tower, San Francisco

P.S. to other readers. Your letters, giving the President and the following Congressmen your opinion in the Redwood National Park crisis, could just do it.

Gossage felt that advertising should be used to raise issues and provoke debate. As Jerry Mander says, to achieve this "he invented that format, that style, that way of speaking and that kind of shocking way of presenting things. ... He liked to throw a pebble in the water and see the ripples."

Gossage remained in charge of the latter but, as far as his commercial clients were concerned, his heart was no longer in it. He was, for example, content to let comedian Stan Freberg write press advertisements and allow Nobel Prize-winning novelist John Steinbeck to consult for Rover Cars.

He still, however, believed in the cause-related work and saw this as the way forward for the agency. However, with his other interests demanding his attention he needed someone who shared his views to take control of that style of advertising. As Alice Lowe says, he was "looking for a successor with a social conscience".[21] And Jerry Mander seemed the perfect candidate.

Jerry Mander certainly appreciated both Gossage's political viewpoint and the way he put it across. As he recalls, "Gossage believed it was possible to use advertising to create issues and cause discussions. Of course, advertisers do that now but they do it with gigantic amounts of money. He would do it with one insertion and a few dollars, and cause big things to happen. He invented that format, that style, that way of speaking and that kind of shocking way of presenting things so that it really broke through .... His advertisements and the ones we did together were highly efficient in that they were actually able to break out a subject or a point of view that had, up until then, not been discussed enough publicly . He was an iconoclast. He said he liked to throw a pebble in the water and see the ripples."[22]

As we've seen in the last chapter, emboldened by the success of the Grand Canyon campaign, Gossage and Mander continued to throw pebbles on behalf of the Sierra Club. Taking all they'd learned, they produced full page, long copy advertisements eliciting support for a 90,000-acre Redwood National Park. One was addressed directly to the president in Washington while another invited readers to send coupons to Ronald Reagan, the governor of California, and the chairmen of the two logging companies that owned the land upon which the park would be created.

More campaigns were to follow. "We did dozens of ads for the Sierra Club on different issues" recalls Jerry Mander. "As well as Redwood National Park there was North Cascades National Park. We did a campaign against the Supersonic Transport landing in the US .... and they were all entirely successful."[23]

The truth ratio

These campaigns were successful despite going head-to-head with opponents with vastly more money to spend on lobbying and advertising. To overcome such odds, they developed what Jerry Mander describes as the "truth ratio". As he explains, "We needed to have 5-10% of the resources of the other side. If we did then we'd win. It we had less than that then we might get really outspent and our stuff wouldn't be visible. But if we had 5-10%, people can recognise the truth when they see it. If you do one truthful ad, it counts for ten of the other guy's. We called it the 'truth ratio.' Gossage was an exponent of that, and I learned it from him."[24]

With each victory, the community that we saw being created by the Grand Canyon campaign grew in numbers, confidence and ambition. And, as each new Sierra Club campaign gained more friends for the cause, then the chief beneficiary was David Brower. For no one shared the nascent Green Movement's ambition, and helped define it better than David Brower. And when Brower launched Friends of the Earth in 1969 it was that community which he and the Gossage agency tapped into.

As we saw in the previous chapter, with little more than Brower's incredible drive and a few newspaper advertisements to promote them, Friends of the Earth went from a three-man outfit working out of the Firehouse to an international organisation within just five years. As Alice Lowe recalls, "Between the agency and Friends of the Earth, Brower's organisation, the Firehouse became the focal point of national conservation activity: it helped small towns with their environmental problems, and it lobbied successfully in Washington DC against much proposed legislation likely to be detrimental to the balance of nature." [25]

Brower and Gossage were perfect partners. For, as the former's mould-breaking Earth National Park advertisement had shown, Brower was not interested in merely saving redwoods and river valleys in the western states of America. He was out to change the world. And, by then, so was Gossage.

Stopping the war

So closely did the two visions converge, and so broadly did they both view their roles, that Brower would eventually brief the agency to create a full page advertisement for Friends of the Earth demanding the withdrawal of all US troops from Southeast Asia. Bold as Brower's ad was, this anti-Vietnam War message had, in fact, already been delivered by Howard Gossage a year earlier.

His effort was prompted by the frustration of seeing a war that he completely opposed being fought in his name. He knew that many others shared his view, so he tried to get that community together and involve them in a collective act of protest. The nature of the mass action was explained in the headline, "Why I am going to: 1) Wear a black tie; 2) Drive with my lights on in broad daylight; & Keep it up until this war is stopped."

Few would describe this as Gossage's greatest advertisement. It does, however, show how far he had come in the few short years since he'd been promoting Pink Air and Eagle Shirts in shades of Unforeseeable Fuchsia. He'd always done things differently, but by the late 'sixties it was barely possible to place his output in the same frame as that of former rivals like Bernbach and Ogilvy.

Ogilvy himself noted the parting of the ways. In his book *Ogilvy on Advertising* he paid tribute to "the most articulate rebel in the advertising business" and his old friend's belief that "advertising was too valuable an instrument to waste on commercial products ... it justified its existence only when it was used for social purposes."[26]

To highlight the difference in their respective commitments to the commercial and social purpose of advertising, let's make one last comparison between the work of these two master copywriters. Both advertisements were written in aid of small, underdeveloped islands in the Caribbean. And both, incidentally, were considered by their authors to be the best ads they ever produced.

Ogilvy's was for Puerto Rico. Under the headline: "Now Puerto Rico offers 100% tax exemption to new industry" it comprised 600 words of fact-filled copy extolling the benefits that industrialists would enjoy when bringing their factories to that poverty-stricken isle.

It was, given the local tax collector's largesse and Ogilvy's prowess, a huge success with over 14,000 people responding. Ogilvy could justifiably have also pointed out that, as well as offering these industrialists a good deal, his advertisement brought the island the important secondary benefits of much needed employment and infrastructural development.

Creating a new country

Gossage, however, would have recognised no merit in such benefits. As we saw in his presentation to the Irish Tourist Board, at the end of Chapter 4, he was already suspicious of inward investment and had tried back then to protect that island from too great a reliance upon tourism and tax breaks to foreign business.

Gossage's opinions hardened and, by the mid-'sixties, he was firmly against smaller, weaker nations becoming dependent upon economic forces beyond their control. Self-sufficiency was the key, and it was this self-sufficient ideal that underpinned Gossage's campaign to help free the tiny Caribbean island of Anguilla.

The people of Anguilla had, in fact, already declared independence from the island federation of which they'd been a member. The British Government frowned upon the break-up of one its Commonwealth dependencies, and started to put pressure upon the Anguillans to get back in line.

It was at this point that Leopold Kohr, Professor of Economics and Public Administration at the University of Puerto Rico, contacted Gossage to enlist his support. Kohr had already done a series of seminars at the Firehouse during which it became clear that his views mirrored those of the adman. When Kohr called Gossage from Puerto Rico, he told him that Anguilla would make the perfect test case for the theories they shared about the twin benefits of smallness and self-sufficiency.

Suitably inspired, Gossage — alongside Dr. Gerald Feigen his partner in Generalists, Inc., TV talk show host and neighbour Arthur Finger, and editor of the *San Francisco Chronicle* Scott Newhall — set up the Anguilla Charter Company aimed at helping the tiny Caribbean island.

All were swept up in the adventure. Arthur Finger, for one, headed off to Anguilla to set up a radio station, and help find college places for the island's brightest children. By his own admission, his was a supporting role to the leading man: Howard Gossage. A still awe-stuck Finger says: "No one I've ever known has been responsible for the creation of a new country."[27]

Nation-building is an expensive business, and to achieve it Gossage and his partners set up a line of credit for $80,000 dollars. Much of it was immediately invested in thousands of silver coins which were shipped over to Anguilla to be used as the new currency. The heads of the breakaway government were then flown to

New York to speak at the United Nations. From New York they were taken to a celebration of independence at the St Francis Hotel in San Francisco for which Alice Lowe was delegated to come up with the catering and Marget Larsen was tasked with running up the new nation's flag.

That sinking feeling

It wasn't, however, going to be that simple. More pressure was exerted by the British and, in response to wavering on the part of the Anguillan leaders and a patronising editorial in the *New York Times,* Gossage sat down and wrote his advertisement. The aim was to stiffen the rebels' resolve, raise some money and, of course, to generate a lot more publicity.

To achieve the latter Gossage did as he always did: write a headline that was designed to create even more headlines. This one read: "Is it 'silly' that Anguilla does not want to become a nation of bus boys?" and argued that the building of just one large hotel would reduce over half the population of 6,000 to servitude.

The money rolled in, and the media spotlight on the island intensified to such a degree that the threat of a bit of latter-day British gunboat diplomacy faded.

So, too, unfortunately did the ideals that had originally inspired the Anguillan rebels. The gunboat looked to be unnecessary when factions formed and rumours circulated that the Anguillan government had made agreements with London and the representatives of international property developers. Not only that, they'd disowned the *New York Times* fundraising advertisement, which left Gossage and his partners open to accusations of fraud.

Gossage immediately went to Anguilla to rally the rebels, only to be told by their president, Ronald Webster, "Well now Howard, I've been thinking it over, and maybe it wouldn't be all that bad an idea to have just maybe one hotel or so".

As Gossage explained, "I blew up. I said that we had financed the whole damned enterprise; we brought their missions to the United States; we paid the bills for their ambassador-at-large and sent a man to help him out. And what have they done? Discredited us. After my speech they handed me a bar check to sign, for $32.

"Then one of the men asked me what I was going to do next. So I told him, 'I'm going to get a great big boat and tow your fucking island out to sea and watch it sink'."[28]

(The Anguilla White Paper)

Is it "silly" that Anguilla does not want to become a nation of bus boys?

THE NEW YORK TIMES, in its editorial of August 7, described the Republic of Anguilla's desperate efforts to remain independent as "touching and silly."

With a pat on the head, the Times advised us to return to the awkward Federation of St. Kitts-Nevis-Anguilla, itself newly formed, from which we had withdrawn shortly after its arbitrary inception on February 27.

We say "arbitrary" because, as you can see from the map, Anguilla does not, even geographically, have much in common with the other two islands. St. Kitts and Nevis are right next door to one another and share a common one-crop, sugar cane, economy dominated by huge, foreign land holdings. Anguilla's land is owned by the islanders themselves; each family has its own little plot and lives off it. Why, then, did Britain lump us in with the other two islands? Because we were their last odd-parcel of real estate in the Caribbean; it's probably that simple. (The Times disregarded these basics, if it ever knew them.)

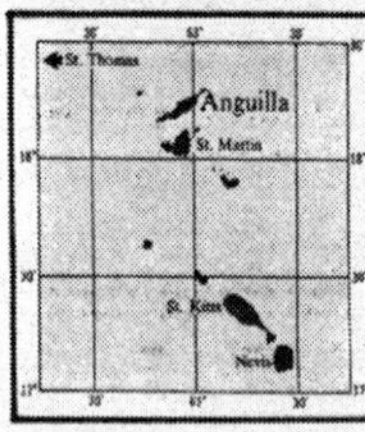

The Times then dismissed our aspirations to independence by pointing out that, "Anguilla has an area of only 35 square miles and a population of 6000. Its people subsist on agriculture and fishing and lack *such modern amenities as telephones.*" (Italics ours.)

This is a terrible indictment in New York eyes, we suppose, but do you know what one Anguillian does when he wants to telephone another Anguillian? He walks up the road and talks to him. Primitive as this arrangement is, it is hardly grounds for justifying the Times' conclusion that Anguilla cannot hope to go it alone.

The fact is that we *have* gone it alone economically, socially, and politically for centuries. The British have neither bothered us, nor bothered about us. We have never been exploited, possibly because there has been nothing much to exploit.

UGLY DUCKLING

To understand this, you must know that Anguilla is referred to in guidebooks as "the ugly duckling of the Caribbean." Objectively that may be so, though to us Anguilla is beautiful because it is our homeland.

There is not enough water on the island for major crop cultivation, nor is it a "tropical paradise"; it is not the prettiest island in the West Indies. The highest point on Anguilla is but 200-and-some-odd feet. There used to be a lot of trees we are told, but these were burned for charcoal long ago. So we must bring in wood to build Anguilla's famous knife-like schooners and sloops.

OLDER THAN U.S.

Anguilla has been left to herself, with generations of the same people, since the 17th century. We are, therefore, a very old nation by any standards. It can even be argued that, as a distinct nation with a stable people, we are older than the United States.

Anguilla is only "new" in the sense that the New York Times had never heard of us before, nor have we had to assert ourselves recently. The last time we were threatened was 250 years ago when the French attempted an invasion with 600 men. They were thrown back by 60 of us, men whose names nearly all Anguillians still bear in direct descent.

There is also this, and it is all-important: Anguilla has proved its self-reliance. It can feed itself, and does. How else do you suppose it could have withstood a blockade—the impounding of our funds, and even our mail—plus the threat of siege by the St. Kitts Government for more than three months now?

"ERRATIC PROCEDURE"

Back to the Times editorial, there is more than a suggestion that Anguillians, though enthusiastic for freedom, are also undisciplined, unrealistic, and given to "erratic procedure." In a word: natives.

We would point out that, whatever the British failed to do on Anguilla, they did give us 300 years of grounding in democratic institutions; and they did establish schools: Anguilla's literacy rate is over 70%, by far the highest in these islands

Which brings us to the Times's unfounded assertion that "there is no truly representative government to speak for the island." That is quite untrue. Anguilla is ruled by a duly elected Council. The premise for this statement was the supposition that Mr. Peter Adams, who has served as a member of the Council, "had a mandate to negotiate for Anguilla" with the British. This is not true either.

Mr. Adams was in the United States seeking help and recognition for us when he, already at the point of exhaustion, enplaned in the middle of the night for Barbados to meet with Great Britain's Minister for Commonwealth Affairs, Lord Shepherd. He flew there from San Francisco arriving after 15 hours of hard travel, with no luggage—only the clothes on his back.

UNREMITTING PRESSURE

It is impossible to know the pressures that were subsequently exerted on this man whom we know to be ordinarily unswerving and extraordinarily dedicated. But after a week, virtually incommunicado toward the end, he submitted to the following demand (in writing) by Lord Shepherd:

> "If you now reject the settlement which we regard as being very reasonable, I must say, in all seriousness, that the British Government cannot continue to countenance the present situation in Anguilla, which constitutes a threat to the stability of the whole Caribbean.
>
> "I shall therefore have to consult with the other Caribbean Governments as to the steps which shall have to be taken to deal with this serious situation."

This "serious situation" was simply that Anguilla, after withdrawing from the embryo Federation in May, had, on July 11, held a plebiscite by secret ballot (above) to confirm its independence beyond question. To insure complete accuracy and believability to the world, this election was supervised, and the ballot count confirmed, by outsiders; correspondents, chiefly.

The returns were embarrassingly lopsided: 1813 For independence, 5 Against. It is therefore utterly impossible that Mr. Adams carried with him what the Times calls "a mandate to negotiate"; i.e., to give up.

BRITISH THREAT NOT EMPTY

Why did he succumb? Well, the British threat of force has seldom been an empty one. Also recall that the St. Kitts government's Prime Minister Bradshaw had, in addition to blocking our mail and our money, threatened—and continues to threaten—our small island with armed force; with no success thus far, though it has meant manning our beaches all night every night for months.

Meanwhile, a British frigate with a force of Royal Marines aboard, lies off our shores. One imagines that the least civil disturbance on Anguilla would serve as a pretext for landing these imposing troops. There is small likelihood of an *internally* induced incident of any kind.

To resume, the Barbados Agreement was immediately declared invalid by the Island Council and by the people themselves in mass meeting. A provisional head of state, Mr. Ronald Webster, was immediately acclaimed pending regular election.

One last insight into why the unfortunate and unauthorized Barbados Agreement calling for Anguilla's return to the St. Kitts-Nevis Federation was signed at all: We do not mean to suggest that melancholy measures were applied to gain assent, but the might and authority of Great Britain—especially when embodied in one who is a high British official *and* a Lord—is not easily ignored after centuries of respect.

WHY WANT US NOW?

It occurs to us that one question may *remain* in American minds. If Anguilla is as we say it is, why would St. Kitts-Nevis, or the British for that matter, wish to bother with us *now*? Well, we *are* somewhat of an affront to what they would regard as fitting and proper; and we are a maddening challenge to Prime Minister Bradshaw's authority over his own troubled domain. The fact that unreachable Anguilla is not troubled by St. Kitts's inherited economic and political ills likely does nothing to allay his discontent; that is only human nature.

But there is another reason, quite new, for finding Anguilla desirable. Anguilla, though unassuming, does have an extremely pleasant climate, cool and dry...and magnificent, untouched beaches. We are "developable."

We could settle our financial distress today were we willing to sign any of the numerous offers we have received from land and resort developers. One company dangled $1,000,000 cash for gambling concessions. We turned it down flatly, despite the anguished realization that this amount of money would underwrite our development for years.

EVEN ONE GREAT HOTEL

Why did we turn these offers down? Because even one magnificent, Hiltonesque hotel on an island of 6000 people, *4000 of whom are youngsters*, would turn us into a nation of bus boys, waiters, and servants.

There is nothing wrong with service or hard physical work, you understand, but a whole *nation* of servants is unthinkable. In five years—or perhaps less—Anguillians would become as sullen, malcontent, and rootless as the rest of the Caribbean; or Harlem, as far as that goes.

Though we haven't mentioned it before, we are a nation of what you would call "Negroes." To us, we are simply Anguillians, because nobody has ever brought the subject up, and that's the way we intend to keep it. But you do see what we mean, don't you? Even one fine hotel and we would become "natives."

HOW LONG CAN WE RESIST?

That brings us up to now. As of this writing the British have not landed troops nor are we given to despair. We still hope for recognition from the United States, from the United Nations, from Great Britain, or from anyone. But if no one chooses to recognize us we shall continue, as we always have, to go it alone.

How long can we hold out? Indefinitely—even without recognition—but we can use temporary financial aid in the meantime.

Our needs are ridiculously small by any standards but our own. For example: our entire island budget—including schools (for those 4000 children)—comes to only $25,000 per month. All our island funds to the amount of $250,000 U.S. are impounded in St. Kitts, yet we have managed.

We have eased the currency shortage somewhat by the issuance of emergency coinage. These "Anguilla Liberty Dollars" are overstamped South American silver dollars, for the most part (see next column).

These coins are being redeemed by friends of Anguilla abroad, and we are putting into circulation the money they fetch.

...TO SURVIVE NOW

It is a little embarrassing for our government to ask you for financial aid on the basis of the unique collateral we have presented here. However, we have no doubt that we will survive this crisis—and do it without selling ourselves out—if we have enough money to survive *now*. We must seek assistance from individuals.

To show our gratitude, we should like to give you something in return, if only to prove that Anguilla is really here and thinking of you even as you think of us.

First off (to disprove the Times's allegation that we don't really have a "representative government"), we had better send you an autographed picture of the Island Council, a facsimile of the original handwritten version of our national anthem, and a small Anguillian flag (a replica of the one now flying over the airstrip). If you wish to help us with as much as $25.00, we'll also send you one of the Anguilla Liberty Dollars.

Those sending $100 or more will become Honorary Citizens of Anguilla. They will receive a document in the form of an Anguillian passport, identical to that which we are issuing to Anguillians, except that it will have an Anguillian Dollar inlaid as shown in the picture. While Americans should not expect to use this passport for foreign travel, it will be good for entering Anguilla. In fact, *only* holders of this passport will be able to visit Anguilla as guests. Why?

In the first place, we have only 30 guest rooms on the entire island at the moment, with no plans to expand. We would not think it either good or polite that so many visitors should be on the island at once that they couldn't at least have lunch with the President. (Besides, since we have such a small population, any more than a very few guests would automatically become "tourists"; we wouldn't want that, and neither would you.)

> **HOW TO SEND CONTRIBUTIONS TO ANGUILLA**
>
> *Since we are cut off from direct postal service—and to give you assurance that your money is safe—an account is being established at the Chase Manhattan Bank on nearby St. Thomas, U.S. Virgin Islands. So please make out your check to: THE ANGUILLA TRUST FUND. And address the letter to: The Anguilla Trust Fund, Chase Manhattan Bank, St. Thomas, U.S. Virgin Islands.*

Thank you for your kind attention during all these troubled weeks, and for hearing us out now, and for your generosity. We won't forget it, or you.

Ronald Webster
Chairman, The Anguilla Island Council

THE NEW YORK TIMES, MONDAY, AUGUST 14, 1967

Gossage didn't write headlines in the Bill Bernbach school i.e. with deft word play that came off the ad's visual. As with his "Anguilla White Paper" ad, he aimed at devising a newsworthy line that would generate even more headlines in the press, and then presenting an elegantly written, impassioned argument that would provoke further comment and controversy.

Introducing anti-globalisation

Independence in itself had never been Gossage's primary concern. His aim was always to establish, as he said, "The sort of homogeneous, self-contained economic social unit that fulfilled Leopold Kohr's ideal political unit: the city-island state."[29] And he was furious with the Anguillan leaders for allowing what he saw as their greed to dismantle his elaborate platform for the professor's ideas.

In truth, they were simply exercising their new-won freedom and opting for a life of relative comfort rather than eking out a living from lobster fishing and salt production. These were the two mainstays of a subsistence economy otherwise dependent on incoming cheques from expatriates working abroad. As for Gossage, you could dismiss his involvement as an exercise in post-colonial meddling – with the white man once again knowing what was best for the newly enfranchised coloured folk.

But, in retrospect, we can also see that Gossage was introducing an argument that is today endorsed by millions of people. Namely that given the financial and environmental cost of importing materials, foodstuffs and, let's not forget, tourists, it is better not to become dependent upon the inflow of foreign goods, foreign capital and foreigners in shorts and bikinis.

Indeed, with an eye to the future, and with the earth's resources getting ever more depleted, it's wiser to encourage local agriculture, fishing, manufacturing and energy, and in so doing create your own community-based economy.

Coming from a man who according to his wife Sally would, for example, only drink imported Veuve Clicquot, rather than the perfectly good fizz produced a few miles away in Napa Valley, this argument might seem a bit rich. But in his own rambunctious way, thirty years before most people had even heard of the word "sustainability", Gossage was articulating the fundamental message of today's large and voluble anti-globalisation movement.

Athough the self-sufficiency ideal was not achieved, Gossage drew immense satisfaction from the advertisement he'd written for Anguilla: "I don't think we realise what a powerful weapon we have in advertising and how much you can do with very little money. This ad in the *New York Times* and in the *Herald Tribune* in Europe together cost $10,000. Well, to do that much with just one ad, and really to do it that inexpensively, is something…. And I think it's very good to be able to exercise our political, our public sentiments in this fashion by our own skills."[30]

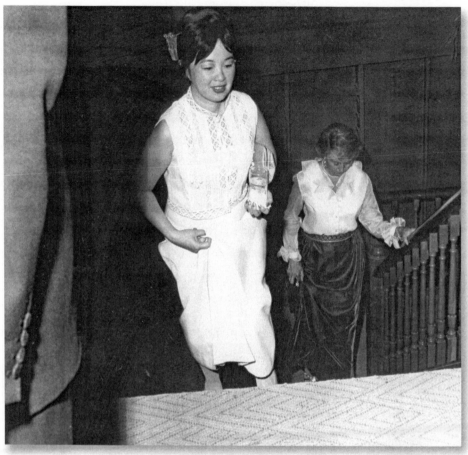

Despite Gossage's frequent trips abroad, many speaking engagements and otherwise hectic schedule, Alice Lowe and Jessica Mitford still managed to squeeze in a spectacular surprise gathering for his 50ᵗʰ birthday on 30 August, 1967. Here is Alice arriving at the event.

One last revolutionary idea

His delight, however real, was short-lived, and not simply because of the ultimate failure of the Anguilla adventure. By the late 'sixties Gossage's time was taken up by frequent trips to Europe, speaking engagements, consultancy work at Generalists, Inc., involvement with *Ramparts* and the arrival of baby daughter, Sarah. Added to this hectic schedule was the launch of perhaps his most radical advertising initiative yet, the Kick-Back Corporation.

As we saw in Chapter 2, advertising agencies made their money from the 15% commission they received when they booked the media in which their advertising

And here at his 50th birthday party are Howard Gossage smoking, Sally emoting and Lewis Lowe, Alice's husband, looking on.

appeared. Gossage opposed this because it rewarded the agency for spending ever-larger amounts on media and relegated the creative product to a giveaway commodity.

In 1957 he rebelled by asking to be paid for the creative work, and then refunding the media commission to the client. In 1967, he delivered another blow to the system with Kick-Back Corporation, the first standalone agency to specialise in buying media.

It was a very shrewd idea. Because buying media was all that Kick-Back did, it wasn't burdened by the massive overheads carried by the advertising agencies. So it could honestly recommend the right media solutions, make a profit and still refund 10% of the normal 15% commission back to the client.

It was also 30 years ahead of its time, because it wasn't until the mid-'90s that the "media independents", as they became known, started to break away from their advertising parents and, in the process, change the industry forever.

Back in 1967, Gossage knew it would cause a ruckus, commenting, "I imagine it will stir up the animals somewhat."[31] He was right. Once again Gossage seemed to be undermining his industry colleagues and *Advertising Age* defended the highly lucrative status quo by initially refusing to run the launch advertisement for the new business.

Bailing-out

Such a response put even more blue sky between Gossage and the industry. As detachment grew and interest dwindled, the need for the old USAF pilot to bail-out became more urgent. Finally, in a letter to Barrows Mussey he wrote, "As of 30 August 1968, my 51st birthday and the 11th anniversary of starting this firm I am retiring the name. From then on it will be Freeman and Mander: they are buying me out. I will be myself from then on ... but not in the business as we know it. But then I haven't been in for some time .... Now, all I have to do is build up a bit more consulting work and I may make as much money as I need for the first consecutive time. But the real kick for me is being able to announce that I am getting OUT."[32]

The official announcement appeared in *Advertising Age* on 3 February, 1969. In it, Gossage explained he had simply lost interest in advertising and was afraid his clients would soon start to notice: "Clients', I believe, living closer to the earth, can sniff this. They have an animal sense, which figures".[33]

He'd also, he said, found "the only person who ever understood what I was up to and is able to do it his own way", Jerry Mander. Gossage continued: "I've always proceeded on the notion that if someone else could do something better than I can, why should I?" And so it continued, with Gossage distancing himself from the agency with every plaudit he aimed in Jerry Mander's direction. When he conceded "I have spent more and more time over the past three years working on things that I give a hoot about", it was clear that *doing* advertising was not and would no longer be one of them.[34]

While announcing the elevation of Jerry Mander, the outgoing head of the agency also mentioned another reason for his decision to step down. He had leukaemia.

Chapter 8

FATAL, BUT
NOT SERIOUS

"IF YOU'RE STUCK
WITH A LEMON,
MAKE LEMONADE"

Howard Gossage had been diagnosed with leukaemia 12 months before his announcement in *Advertising Age* and had, in fact, initially been given only six months to live. In the face of adversity he'd always been the supreme pragmatist, summing up his philosophy with the aphorism, "If you're stuck with a lemon, make lemonade".[1] True to form, he managed to make the best of even this most dreadful piece of news.

As he wrote to Bob McLaren, the English creative director whom he'd met on his first trip to Germany, "Funny thing is, it didn't bother me at all. I turned into a real dynamo (You feel immortal, let's say really alive.)"[2]

The grim prognosis also brought a distinct advantage. As he told Dugald Stermer, "The doctor has given me six months to live, so in that six months you will do exactly what I want you to do."[3]

Bravery and black humour aside, as Alice Lowe says, he genuinely believed he "was going to lick it", and when his doctors revised and extended their original six month deadline, he looked forward to a long period of remission.[4] In his September 1968 letter to Bob McLaren he wrote, "It's one of those things that are fatal but not serious, if you follow me. I'm in great shape, probably good for another 20-30 years. No shit."[5]

If that was the case then having, in his view, wasted so much of his time in advertising, he wasn't going to fritter away this second chance.

Jugs of lemonade

Gossage's great friend, Warren Hinckle, described him as an intellectual dedicated to "the creation and also the propagation of good ideas"[6]. Jerry Mander said, he was ever "in search of the elegant solution to life's problems".[7] Somewhere between the two, it seems, lay the course of Gossage's new life.

To begin with, he was finally going to get down to writing the book that publishers Little, Brown had commissioned from him years earlier.

He and Dr. Gerald Feigen, his partner in Generalists, Inc., then started planning a series of lectures on Mediatrics – or (with typical foresight) what "middle age" meant in a society where increasingly that term applied to anyone in the 35-75 age group. There was much media interest. NBC proposed a documentary on the

HOWARD LUCK GOSSAGE
451 Pacific, San Francisco

6 May 1969

Dear Mr. Oakes —
I just got a list of those dear people who had contributed blood to me. I was much touched to find your name on the (really quite short) list. (It is apparently the sort of thing one talks about more than does.) You did it and I am most grateful.
Thank you again,
Howard Gossage

Gossage had numerous transfusions, and asked for a list of those who had donated the blood. In May 1969, when even the act of holding a pen had become excruciating, he insisted on sending each of them a handwritten "thank you" note.

subject, and *Esquire* magazine said they were going to dedicate a 10,000 word feature article about its main spokesman, Gossage.

Contemplating a big jug of freshly made lemonade, Gossage told Barrows Mussey, "I'm tempted to think a lot of this interest stems from the leukemia. I know it sure as hell hasn't hurt anything".[8]

Keen to turn that interest into something beneficial to others, Gossage planned writing and paying for a full-page press advertisement that would invite fellow-sufferers to share their experiences. Such communities are commonplace nowadays on the internet but, back in 1969, the idea was typically way ahead of its time.

On a more personal level Gossage, who was undergoing frequent blood transfusions, also asked Alice Lowe for a full list of all the donors, so he could write a note of thanks to each one of them.

The guru discoverers

Given his long list of "things to do", it's little wonder Gossage was keen to announce his retirement from advertising.

A month before that announcement appeared in *Advertising Age*, Gossage set about doing for Leopold Kohr, his partner in the Anguilla adventure, what he had done for Marshall McLuhan. He had high hopes that this would be another hit and sent Barrows Mussey a note saying "I think he is about to happen the same way McLuhan did."[9]

Having invested $6,000 in launching McLuhan and taken out an astronomical $80,000 loan trying to prove Kohr's theory in Anguilla, Gossage and his consulting partner Dr. Gerald Feigen, finally decided to get someone else to pick up the tab – and start making some money themselves

The plan was to set up a Seminar Foundation and get interested sponsors to pay $5,000 or $10,000. As Gossage said, "$5,000 isn't much for a corporation hoping to make a big splash with a new idea or a new approach or a new guru. We are guru discoverers. And for that money you can get ... almost any first class person in the world." When he concluded "you can skin it for $10,000 easy – and still make a tidy profit," there were signs that, under threat of fatal illness,

HOWARD LUCK GOSSAGE

451 PACIFIC, SAN FRANCISCO

8 March 1968

Dear Mussey,

Thank you for the check. This does not entirely cover
your request for an answer to your mail, I realize. Nor
did I intend to be evasive when I was talking to you on
the phone yesterday. It just that a lot has happened.

As with my health. I got home to find I have leukemia
and was about two quarts low blood blood-wise, which is
enough to enervate anyone. It's a wonder I didn't fall
dead from all that running around I was doing. It's
no wonder I looked a bit pale. My reaction to this
interesting news was typical of a man who has delighted
in finding lemons to make lemonade out of-- I was elated:
just to think, I said, here I am alive (one generally
doesn't realize this outside of the Reader's Digest). And
I have used it like a bludgeon to get things done. I have
never been one to harbor secrets and why start now. The
worst I can see happen is that it will drive up the price
of my services, which now may or may not be in short long-
range supply. I just don't know; they have great luck in
arresting the disease (the dandiest form of cancer I do
believe) and I seem to be responding splendidly. Well,
my ebullience about it all has made it quite easy to bear
for Sally and my spirits have been splendid. I feel
great. Tell Dag to stop that caterwauling; I may have 20
years. Total remissions are quite common nowadays.
About that trip to Burdaville -- and Gstaad-- they were in
connection with Ramparts. They want to print over there
and somehow pull Burda into the deal--projected plans
about establishing a new news magazine, but only in
an international edition published in europe in English.
The Gstaad portion of the trip was money raising from a
rich American millionaire there. Ramparts, as usual, is
eking it out.

I have not had time to do anything about the book. At first
-- before I found I was responding-- the thought of post-
houmous publishing was not vastly urgent-making. Now I
shall plow ahead. I guess. My first concern is to make a
great deal of money, and to do that I shall have to put
a Greater Shade Tree together. That electronics firm
Pressman spoke of might be a good thing to acquire-- along
with Ramparts for the tax loss-- and then some other
notions. It's just conceivable I could turn the whole
thing into one of the great glamour stocks of our time.
Kelso is about to materialize here and I am going to start
exploring. I'll let you know, certainly, for you figure
in, of course.

Love, Howard

*From this letter to Barrows Mussey, we get an insight into Gossage's remarkably sanguine approach to the news of his illness.
We can also see that he was assuming a much more business-like approach to the new life he saw spanning out before him.*

the man whose business plan had previously been "play it fat, dumb and happy" was suddenly being rather prudent.[10]

In fact, upon hearing of his illness he'd told Barrows Mussey, "My first concern is to make a great deal of money."[11] No doubt this was driven by the need to provide financial security for wife Sally and baby daughter Sarah – and his two other children, Eben and Amy, from an earlier marriage. But perhaps it also indicated that a man who'd always been ahead of the cultural curve was jettisoning the nonacquisitive values that had become so fashionable by the late 'sixties.

If that appears fanciful, then just consider the electro-hippies we met in Chapter 5 and how they ultimately had no problem reconciling their genuine idealism with the making of a fabulous profit. Moreover, let's look to Gossage's friend, and that shrewd interpreter of the *zeitgeist*, Tom Wolfe. In the early 'seventies he created his character "The man who always peaked too soon." Viewed with today's 20/20 hindsight, it is clear to see how this proponent of materialism provided readers with a prescient preview of the outlook that would be required in a more pragmatic decade.[12]

Speaking of pragmatism, in his letters to Mussey, Gossage spoke of ambitious plans to buy an electronics company and turn his Shade Tree organisation into a diversified portfolio of businesses. In fact, in one of those letters, he even invited Mussey to head up the European branch of Shade Tree.*

If he aimed at building a business empire, then it would be commercial imperialism spread by an eccentric bunch of renegades. Foremost amongst them was the buccaneering Warren Hinckle who, when *Ramparts* finally faced bankruptcy, was set up by Gossage in the Firehouse as editor of an even more radical left wing magazine, *Scanlan's*.

Gossage who hated the idea of any book, however bad, being destroyed, was also working with Hinckle on a business buying, packaging and re-selling library

---

*The new business-like approach wasn't totally dominant and the fun-loving, big-spending Gossage often reasserted himself. When his illness got too oppressive he would invoke "the cancer clause, which is be extravagant i.e. normal".[13] In November 1968, for example, he was working in Chicago which he figured was far enough east to justify a trip to Ireland. Actually, the Irish trip lasted just one day, and was merely a pretext for him and Sally to spend four days cruising there and another four days cruising back on one of their favourite liners, the *Nieuw Amsterdam*.

books which were otherwise destined for pulping. True to his expansionist plans, he offered Barrows Mussey the option of distributing in Germany.

Meanwhile, Gossage aimed to publish the work of the gurus that he and Dr. Feigen were unearthing. With Barrows Mussey, who had originally put them on to Kohr, enthusiastically helping in the search, they considered such academic luminaries as philosopher Suzanne Berger and political economist Louis Orth Kelso. They actually "launched" Kelso at a party in New York in March 1968 but ultimately Gossage was unimpressed and concluded, "Leopold is the only decent one of the lot, but he is the only one who ever got us into trouble. That man has a built-in fucked-upness. He can't ask for directions to the men's room without making such a batch of confusion for Feigen and me that we feel like punching him in the eye. Witness Anguilla."[14]

"Built-in fucked-upness" aside, Gossage had great respect for Kohr's thinking. As he said, "The only one who believes his theories and acts on them is me."[15]

Doing a McLuhan on Leopold Kohr

Kohr was an Austrian economist, lawyer and political scientist who contended that pretty much all the sins of the world could be ascribed to the cult of bigness. Whether it was the nation state, the corporation or the city, the bigger they got the more unwieldy, inefficient and inhumane they became. Hence his interest in Anguilla and his attempts to establish it as an independent island state that existed in self-sustaining isolation from the outside world.

Gossage had run his business on a similar principle. According to Alice Lowe, "The economist pointed out that Howard had effectively created a miniature city-state in the Firehouse – he had gathered together a group of people of diverse skills who enjoyed each other's company; by working together, they were able to create a good life for themselves; and by keeping within the physical limitations of the Firehouse they had avoided the problems of over-expansion."[16]

So what Kohr had to say certainly made sense to Gossage. In fact, just as McLuhan had taken the original premise of feedback and interaction and theorised it into a way of improving humankind, so Kohr was taking the smallness principle that had so informed Gossage's life and work, and was translating it into a utopian ideal.

Whilst nothing like as sensational as McLuhan's launch, Leopold Kohr's promotional tour to Houston and New York had an impact that lives with us today. His book, *The Breakdown of Nations* (1957) and other writings went on to inspire the "small is beautiful" movement – most commonly associated with Kohr's protégé, E.F.Schumacher. In so doing he has influenced everyone from the most liberal environmentalist to the most reactionary survivalist. Anyone in fact who, like Howard Gossage, dreaded the dehumanising effects of big business, big bureaucracies and big government.

One more broadside

You can add to Gossage's list of pet hates, "big media." And, in May 1969, he returned to the pages of *Advertising Age* with a passionate jeremiad about its inherent dangers. Under a typically long, provocative headline: "Advertising has tremendous (unwanted) economic power and here are things it should do about it", Gossage explained that "the single most powerful propaganda medium the world has ever seen controls all our mass media."[17]

Warming to his theme Gossage said that advertising's "control over content" was responsible for the "dreary sameness of broadcasting". Not only that, but because newspaper and magazine owners had become reliant upon the revenue they received from advertisers, those advertisers were using their spending power to control and, worse still, close down the nation's publications. As he pointed out, "Over half our metropolitan newspapers have died, not because their readers didn't want them, but because advertisers didn't."[18]

Gossage had an instant remedy. He argued for the readers of newspapers to pay the full price that it cost to produce the 'paper and thus free the 'papers' owners from their dependence upon advertising. Back in the late 'sixties, what he termed "Pay Reading" seemed too drastic to those who'd gotten used to having the newsstand price subsidised by the advertising that interrupted, and dictated, the editorial content.[19]

Yet forty years later Gossage's Pay Reading idea of a medium free from advertising control is writ large in the most exciting and respected TV channel on the US airwaves. And one suspects that if Howard Gossage were alive today he'd happily pay the monthly subscription in order to enjoy the unadulterated delights of HBO.

Back, however, to the adulterated TV of the late 'sixties and Gossage couldn't resist using this appearance in *Advertising Age* to fire another broadside at advertising's boring and bombastic content. Careful to avoid hitting the smaller, nimbler creative craft that were now bobbing around on the airwaves, he aimed directly at his old target, the industry's stately galleons: "The industry tries to pretend that the incidents (of bad taste) are few and far between ... committed by fringe or fly-by-night operators. It just isn't true; they happen all the time, and the bulk of intelligence-insulting, banal, tasteless advertising is done by the biggest agencies for the biggest clients."[20]

Coming out of retirement

Having renewed his battle with his old adversaries, Gossage came out of retirement to show them how it was done. Fittingly enough, the advertisement's aim was, quite literally, the saving of the planet.

The client was publishing house Harpers & Row, which was promoting its book: *ABM: An Evaluation of the Decision to Deploy an Anti-Ballistic Missile System.* Clearly they were taking the book's launch seriously. Not only had they spent $40,000 on space in the *New York Times, Boston Globe, Chicago Tribune, Washington Post, Minneapolis Tribune,* and *Los Angeles Times,* they'd also shifted the assignment to Gossage from their agency of record, Denhard & Stewart.

It was the toughest of assignments for, by then, to use Alice's Lowe's poignant understatement, the disease "was gaining on Howard".[21] It was now fatal, and very serious. However, although he was weakened by the cancer, and crippled by the cortisone he was taking to alleviate his pain, he went at it with typical flair.

With a bold, mould-breaking flourish, his headline ran to 56 words over one page and continued onto a second page. The body copy then took up the argument against the US government's decision to deploy that ultra-sophisticated offshoot of Norbert Wiener's Statistical Predictor, the Anti-Ballistic Missile (ABM) system.

Gossage pointed out the frightening complexity of the ABM system, and its error-prone mix of missiles, computers and radars. Fact after fact was deployed with characteristic elegant indignation, culminating in a couponed call to action aimed at getting people to vote "YES" or "NO" on whether they felt their family would be safe with the Safeguard ABM System.

In the body copy Gossage had written: "It is necessary for the people in whose names these creations are introduced to remind the government that we do not wish to abdicate our right of control and approval merely because we don't understand the technology right off. We do understand the consequences."

True to the interactive Gossage style, this would no doubt have been the first of several advertisements aimed at allowing the people to reassert their "right of control and approval". It was, however, one conversation that he was never able to develop.

Precious jade

Four weeks after this advertisement appeared, Alice Lowe got a call from her boss. "I remember distinctly what he said: 'For the first time in my life Alice, I feel completely free. I've gotten completely out of the advertising business – Jerry Mander's going to be taking care of that – I'll be able to do anything I want from now on.' He was so weak, he could barely whisper." [22]

Two days later, Dr. Gerald Feigen advised Alice to take her last chance to see him. Whilst together, the man who'd so craved affection as a young boy told her, "You know Presh, I have a whole new family outside of the one I was born into and the ones I've raised. It's you and Warren and Jerry. Warren is like a brother to me, a pal; Jerry is like a son, the heir to the agency; and you, you're like a sister." [23] Alice recalls, "I slipped a small piece of jade into his hand, and explained that in China people believe that stroking the stone helps bring peace to the spirit. 'Thank you, Presh', he said, 'you've always understood me.' He looked tired. As I rose to go, he waved goodbye, jade in hand." [24]

Howard Gossage died at 4.30 the following morning.

A different agency to the very end

The date was 9 July. By the end of that month, 1969 had already seen the launch of nearly 100 new advertising agencies in the United States.[25] In August, the "Creative Revolution" was headlining on the cover of *Newsweek*, and its poster girl, Mary Wells, was ousting her partner at Wells, Rich, Greene and emerging as the highest paid executive in advertising earning $250,000 a year.[26]

In an industry awash with money, Gossage's former partners were left with the question of what to do with the agency now that its founder and figurehead was gone.

As Alice Lowe explains, both she and Jerry Mander knew they could capitalise upon the association with Gossage, and sell the business. Howard Gossage had, after all, been a major player in the industry and, although small, his agency was held in high regard and would have been coveted by the larger networks who were always on the lookout for new acquisitions.

The sudden explosion of start-ups and the creative revolution that it generated would also have made an agency like his an even more attractive proposition to the Madison Avenue giants. For the acquisition of one of the original hot shops would, by association, have enhanced their creative credentials.

Alice and Jerry knew they could get a high price for bringing a patina of creative credibility to a Young & Rubicam or a Ted Bates.

They realised, however, that there would also be a price to pay. As Alice Lowe says, "Jerry and I, the more we talked, the more we felt that you can't control anything once you sell it. No matter what the intentions are of the people who buy it .... We knew that once you're on their payroll you may have to take some accounts you wouldn't otherwise take, because you have to meet the payroll and other things. So we decided that for Howard's reputation and the agency's reputation Jerry and I were firmly against selling and said 'let's just dissolve it'. So we did and I'm sure that Jerry and I never regretted that because if anything had come out of there that was not up to standard we would have been sick about it. So, we walked away without a penny to our names. Which is OK because you don't do that sort of thing for money."[27]

That final remark, "You don't do that sort of thing for money" is worth repeating because it's a last and poignant expression of Gossage's original intention to start a new kind of agency.

Back in the 'fifties and 'sixties (and even more so today) the primary reason to start an agency was the promise of a big pay-off when the time came to sell. Which means Howard Gossage's agency defied convention even as it passed into history.

Or more accurately, obscurity.

There was, it is true, a respectful obituary in *Advertising Age* titled "Sometimes Funny, Sometimes Poignant – Always Disturbingly Trenchant". But that was basically it, and within a handful of years Gossage, the showman who craved attention and needed the spotlight, was forgotten by the advertising industry he'd illuminated through-out his career.*

Aftermath

To those who shared Gossage's liberal views, it must have seemed like just another instance of darkness descending.

In politics, the gunning down of Dr. Martin Luther King, Jr. and Bobby Kennedy proved there'd be "no happy-ever-aftering" in any kind of political Camelot. In music, the "come together" idealism of the Trips Festival and subsequent Summer of Love was killed by the pool cue and knife-wielding Hell's Angels at Altamont. And, as for the Whole Earth Catalog-reading hippies, well in August 1969 they saw how easy it was for their countercultural sense of community to mutate into something as truly alternative as the Manson Family.

Add to that the death of an adman who wanted to harness advertising's power for the greater good, and you can see that, at the end of the 'sixties, left-leaning liberals were stuck with plenty of lemons from which to make some pretty bitter lemonade.

Gossage's former partners seemed to realise that the carefree days of playing it "fat, dumb and happy" were long gone.

---

*Correction. There was a flash of posthumous limelight when, ten months after his death, Gossage became only the tenth person to be inducted into the Copywriters Hall of Fame by the Copy Club of New York. Others previously honoured included David Ogilvy, Bill Bernbach and, yes, Rosser Reeves.

Alice Lowe, exhausted by the effort of ensuring that the agency balanced its books before closing its doors, left advertising, and for the past 40 years has applied her prodigious organising skills and creative flair to the needs of the Asian Art Museum of San Francisco. Jerry Mander, ever true to his principles, abandoned commercial advertising for good. Instead, he started Public Interest Communications, the first agency to specialise in not-for-profit clients. Since then he has dedicated his life to warning of, and fighting against, the effects of globalisation.

For their part, Marget Larsen and Bob Freeman set up their design business, Intrinsics, in a small office a few blocks away from the Firehouse. It was there that a young copywriter called Jeff Goodby discovered them, and Howard Gossage, ten years later.

Regaining the spotlight

As Goodby says, "In the early 'eighties no one knew about Gossage. It was strange. There was a gap in everybody's memory."[28]

It's not so strange really. Like its contemporary counterpart, the Maoist Cultural Revolution which sought to obliterate vast tracts of Chinese history, the creative revolution, with its burgeoning cult of Chairman Bill, bred a similar contempt for the past.

With a self-assured ignorance that remains uncorrected to this day, young creatives figured they had nothing to learn, and developed an historical perspective that stretched back only to the last major awards show. Their elders stayed silent and followed fashion for fear of being denounced as reactionary or, that most unforgivable sin in the advertising business, old.

Thankfully Jeff Goodby, fellow copywriter Andy Berlin and art director Rich Silverstein were willing to think beyond the new orthodoxy. These three young admen had been assigned by their boss Hal Riney to promote the San Francisco Advertising Awards, and they'd decided to create a category that honoured "Copywriting". It was Goodby's idea to name it after a famous old-timer and one Bay Area veteran said, "How about Howard Gossage?"[29]

None of the three had heard the name before but were told that two of "this guy Gossage's" former colleagues still worked in the city. And so the three young creatives went round to the old folks' small office and were greeted by Marget Larsen and Bob Freeman, who were more than happy to share their stories.

As Goodby says, out of that meeting grew a friendship between himself, Berlin and Silverstein; a respect for Larsen and Freeman; and a love affair with the Gossage way of doing things. Indeed, when Goodby, Berlin and Silverstein set up their own agency in 1983 they launched with a headline that paid tribute to their mentor, "Introducing a new agency founded by a guy who died 14 years ago." Nearly 30 years later and Rich Silverstein is still clear about the agency's inspiration, "Is it true that Gossage was the reason we founded our company? Yes."[30]

Meanwhile, Gossage's admirers in Europe were keeping the faith. Although Barrows Mussey died in 1985, the book he did so much to create: *Ist die Werbung noch zu retten? (Can Advertising be Saved?)* was, under his wife Dagmar's determined supervision, reprinted in Germany, and finally published for an English-speaking audience as *Is There Any Hope for Advertising?* in 1986. The torch was taken up in 1995 by Bruce Bendinger when he published his homage, *The Book of Gossage*. Those who have read it are left in no doubt that the man's legacy was far richer than that of Mary Wells — and her $250,000 annual salary — or any of the other Mad Men whose fame eclipsed his in the 'fifties, 'sixties and the years thereafter.

The epitaph he dreaded (revisited)

Would he have liked the comparison? Probably not because, as we've seen, he had little interest in his peers, and even less respect for the industry in which they all worked. Given his disdain, it is tempting to think of Gossage as a brilliant man who just happened to be in advertising. But to do so would be to ignore a truth that would probably have annoyed the hell out of him: he was a marketing genius with a gift for writing great ads.

Rory Sutherland, a long-term devotee and now vice-chairman of the UK Ogilvy Group puts him in context: "Gossage is the Velvet Underground to Ogilvy's Beatles and Bernbach's Stones. Never a household name but, to the cognoscenti, a lot more inspirational and influential."[31] A leader of the Gossage cognoscenti, Jeff Goodby, agrees, "The best of Gossage is the best advertising ever done."[32]

An overstatement? Well, in his book *The Real Mad Men*, Andrew Cracknell tries to get the reader to appreciate the brilliance of Bill Bernbach's output. But, however outrageous running a page advertisement with a headline that spelt BARGAINS backwards might have been in the '50s, it comes across as a "you had to be there" moment to today's audience.[33]

Gossage's long copy headline for Fina, however, would still be outstanding. For who today would have the audacity to write something as arrestingly irreverent as "If you're driving down the road and you see a Fina station and it's on your side so you don't have to make a U-turn though traffic and there aren't six cars waiting and you need gas or something please stop in."

In this and other campaigns, he created a new style of interactive advertising and, in Jeff Goodby's, words "foretold what's happening in the internet and social media".[34] That alone should be sufficient to win him universal respect. But the ads were just one aspect of his brilliance.

As we've seen, he was the first adman to recognise the marketing potential in what Daniel J. Boorstin had identified as the "Pseudo-event". Fifty years later, and all today's big PR-generating campaigns that are lionised at the Cannes Advertising Festival for their ground-breaking brilliance can be traced to Gossage's ad platform technique. None, however, will ever be as ambitious as his Anguilla campaign. As we saw in the last chapter, for Gossage it wasn't primarily about freeing the people of that island. It was a dramatisation of Leopold Kohr's theories done on a scale that no PR or marketing campaign had attempted before or since.

Ultimately it didn't work but, in marketing terms, never was there a more glorious failure.

Other of his innovations had to wait decades to find success. The Kick-Back Corporation (the first media-only agency), Generalists, Inc., (which pioneered what we now call behavioural economics) and Pay Reading (which comes to us today as Pay per View); all were big marketing ideas that singly should have guaranteed lasting recognition. Taken together, they're evidence of marketing genius.

It is true that he would not have liked that conclusion. Indeed, he preferred the company of more esoteric thinkers, and looked for the kind of cause that he felt more worthy of his talent and intellect. But the truth, like his destiny, was inescapable: he had a lonely boy's need for an audience and a vaudevillian's natural ability to enthrall them. And the two came together in advertising.

Rugged individualist

As to worthy causes, his achievements can be measured in his determination to create something new and daring in the Firehouse on Pacific Avenue ... the way he applied feedback and information loops to advertising to create a more humane, involving alternative ... how he used both to get to a rudimentary form of interactive and social media ... the way they came together in his Grand Canyon campaign, and how that led to the creation of the vast and ever-growing community, the Green Movement ... his discovery and promotion of Marshall McLuhan, the man behind the men who brought us Twitter, Facebook and digital utopianism ....

But let's stick there on "utopianism". For that is what Gossage ultimately stood for: the betterment of mankind through original thought and sometimes, when necessary, courageous action. That was his worldview, his politics.

And if all politics are ultimately personal, and the true test of a man's worth isn't what he says in general but what he does in particular, then how did his talk about "changing the world" stack up with his behaviour to individuals around him?

Well, strangely enough for a progressive left-leaning liberal, he sought to live his life like that traditional paragon of American Conservative politics and popular culture, the rugged individualist: the loner who rides into town and betters the lives of the people through the strength of his conviction and the skill at his disposal.

Gossage aimed to be that "can do" hero. He firmly believed that he should involve himself in the lives of others, and help make things better for them. If there was a problem, he hated dwelling on its causes, or what *should* have happened. Instead, as his friend Warren Hinckle recalled, "he'd shrug and say, 'You can't stop dogs peeing on fire hydrants'", and then get on with sorting things out.[35]

Nowadays, we've lost faith in this kind of altruistic individualism, and are only too willing to abdicate personal responsibility to the State or whatever institution we feel is supposed to be taking care of us. Indeed, we've surrendered so fully to the culture of dependence that we're now threatened by, and suspicious of, those who don't bow to the general mood of apathetic fatalism.

Making people better

This is another form of consumerism that Gossage would have hated. And certainly one he would never have conformed to. As Alice Lowe says, "Howard had absolute faith that an intelligent person, given a choice, would elect to be generous rather than selfish." In fact, Gossage felt that the intelligent, sentient individual had no real choice in the matter at all. As he explained, "That's the terrible thing about responsibility, once you recognise it, it's yours. The only way to escape this inexorable law is to be dumb or unconscious." [36]

This sense of responsibility shaped his life. As his wife Sally recalls, "He wanted to fix things, he wanted to make everything and everybody better."[37]

We've already seen how this led to his part-time career as a "guru hunter." As he acknowledged, "What I can really do, I can convince these gurus like Marshall McLuhan and Leopold Kohr that their ideas will actually work."[38]

But Gossage did much more than provide career guidance to the intellectually very gifted. He was interested in everybody. As Sally continues, "He was always bringing in some young guy that he saw some spark in, and he would bring it out and then send them happily on their way, and rejoice in their success." [39]

Dugald Stermer was one such "young guy". When Gossage met him in Texas he told him "you need to escape Houston", and rescued him by getting him a job at first Neiman Marcus and then as art director on *Ramparts* magazine.[40]

It was the first of many increasingly prestigious appointments as Stermer went on to become one of the most respected designers of his generation, the creator of the medals at the 1984 Los Angeles Olympics, and art director and editorial illustrator for such magazines as *Harpers, Rolling Stone, GQ, Time* and *Esquire*. In short, a brilliant, illustrious career, and one which Stermer happily concedes would never have happened without Gossage. As he says, "His whole life was about finding people and then discovering what it was they wanted to do. And then making it possible for them to do it. That's what he was about."[41]

Founding Florence

Dugald Stermer's colleague on *Ramparts*, Bob Scheer, would agree: "He was a liberating figure. He gave us encouragement and, whereas others would say you're not going to survive, he was on our side. We weren't *Time* magazine, we didn't have the big bucks but we all knew this was an important venture and we were trying to do significant journalism. He gave us the confidence to believe we could pull it off.

"He wasn't threatened by anything that was going on. He risked his reputation and was critical to the whole venture. I never could figure out what was in it for him. It certainly wasn't that he was making any money out of it. Looking back, it's rare that you find a really selfless man; yet Gossage was willing to give us a shot just because we were trying to make a difference."[42]

Bob Scheer has carried on trying to make a difference since those formative days with Gossage at *Ramparts*. He went on to write for the *Los Angeles Times* from 1976 until 2005 when his need to stir up the controversial mush got him fired. He then moved on-line to become editor-in-chief of *Truthdig* which has brought him four Webby awards for best political blog, and confirmed his reputation as one of America's greatest radical journalists of the past half-century.

His appreciation for Gossage as patron and mentor remains undiminished. As he says, "He was the kind of guy who, if he'd had a lot of money, could have founded Florence or some place like that – but he didn't, so he did it with his personality instead." [43]

The young Jay Conrad Levinson was another beneficiary. He started as Gossage's secretary in the early months of Weiner & Gossage, taking down and then typing up his boss's dictation. Gossage encouraged the former G.I. to try his hand at writing and each morning Levinson would leave his effort on Gossage's desk, and wait nervously for the response. Time and again, he'd get his copy back covered in notes and comments. Then, one day, the sheet came back unmarked and the advertisement was allowed to run.

At this juncture, most bosses would have capitalised upon the months of tuition by taking the tyro on staff and hiring out his skills to clients at a sizeable margin. Not Gossage. As Levinson recalls, he said, "It's now time for you to go and be a copywriter on your own."[44] Levinson's next job paid him five times more than his previous salary. And the benefits of his training continued thereafter. With his *Guerrilla Marketing* series of books, which have sold over 20 million copies and been translated into 62 languages, and his worldwide speaking engagements, he has become the most successful advertising consultant of his generation.

Across the generations

Levinson, who cites Gossage as the one who introduced the idea of "Guerrilla Marketing", isn't alone in saying, "I owe so much to Howard".[45]

As we've seen, another advertising luminary, Jeff Goodby came under the influence long after his hero's death. According to him, "He was a magnetic, giving character, the hub of a wheel of people who were all interesting …. He was an enabler for them. A lot of them talk about how he was a creative spark, a fun guy to be with because he would make you better. I think that was one of his secrets. Howard enabled people like that and, in a funny way, he did it for me down across a generation."[46]

You can make that two generations if you take into account the massive influence that Gossage had on Alex Bogusky.

As creative partner at Crispin Porter + Bogusky, he produced advertising of a standard unmatched anywhere in the world for much of the period 1995-2010. Unmatched, that is, by anyone but Gossage forty years earlier.

As Bogusky says, "You really can't overstate the influence of Gossage on the early CPB work. At one point every new hire was given a copy of *The Book of Gossage* … to the core group it was a touchstone. As our work began to move online we used to sit around and wonder, "What would Gossage do? WWGD? In some ways it was an exercise but in another way we really felt like he would have enjoyed the new medium as much as we were. Online advertising at the time was rarely interactive in the literal sense, and every day was an opportunity for us to illustrate what it could be. We almost felt a responsibility to be interactive in the shadow of Howard." [47]

The cornerstone of my life

The same indebtedness to Gossage's influence, and the same need to honour his memory has informed the life and career of Hubert Burda. As we saw in the last chapter, Gossage befriended the young Burda during his trips to Germany and then escorted him round the leading advertising agencies and publishing houses in New York and Chicago. As Dr. Burda, as he now is, says, "You can really describe him as the cornerstone of my life, we were like father and son .... He taught me that making money in business is not enough. People want to say 'we work in a company that has higher goals'. This is the altruistic feeling that Howard had."[48]

Hubert's empathy for what he called Howard Gossage's "higher social engagement" has turned the Burda Media empire into a global force for good.[49] Amongst his many sponsorships of the arts, literature, science and technology are the Burda Academy for the Third Millennium founded as an inter-disciplinary forum for specialists in culture and science; The Felix Burda Foundation set up in 2001 to research the prevention of intestinal cancer; the *Iconic Turn* lectures focusing on the impact of technological change on society; the Hubert Burda Center for Innovative Communications at the Ben Gurion University in Beer Sheva, Israel; and his active support for Steven Spielberg's Shoah Foundation, the world's most extensive collection of reports by Holocaust survivors and other witnesses.

Looking back to his time with Howard Gossage, Dr. Burda says "I hope I haven't disappointed him."[50] He needn't worry, for Gossage would have delighted in his efforts. As Tom Wolfe says, "Howard was a person who somehow imparted a fantastic energy to anything that people around him wanted to undertake ... . He somehow made you able to soar a little higher and to do it with a kind of zest for your own life that you probably had not had before ... . At the same time, he exulted in whatever other people could do with their lives. In fact, that was the one thing that Howard insisted on – that you somehow get on the Dionysian plane with him, and if you could do it, no one would applaud louder than Howard. It was a dare that he handed you, a dare that I will certainly never forget."[51]

Nor will Alice Lowe, who herself soared a little higher when, as we saw in Chapter 2, Gossage enthusiastically encouraged her to study to become a docent at San

Francisco's Asian Art Museum. Alice really did become his "contribution to culture" when, in 1989, she became the first Chinese-American to be elected Chairperson of that august institution.

From encountering a downhearted Gossage on the day he flunked the job interview with Joe Weiner in 1953 to comforting him on the night of his death in 1969, Alice Lowe knew the man longer than anyone else. So, we'll leave the last words to her: "He believed in people and somehow, through the strength of his conviction, made them believe in themselves and made them willing to strive for difficult goals which they thought unattainable. He made them think and instilled them with the courage to try."[52]

In so doing, he not only shaped the lives of those around him, but also changed the world we live in today. An admirable legacy, yes, but as he told Dugald Stermer, "the only fit work for a grown man".[53]

NOTES

Introduction

1 Stephen Fox, *The Mirror Makers: A History of American Advertising and its Creators* (New York, 1997; first published, New York, 1984), p.173
2 Martin Mayer, *Madison Avenue U.S.A.* (London, 1961; first published, New York, 1958), p.39
3 Stephen Fox, p.20
4 Jim Ellis, *Billboards to Buicks: Advertising as I Lived It* (London, New York and Toronto, 1968), p.11
5 Stephen Fox, p.217
6 *Penn State Journal*, "How to Want to do Better Advertising", January, 1963

Chapter 1

1 Interview with Sally Kemp, 12 November, 2010
2 Interview with Dugald Stermer, 18 November, 2010
3 Interview with Sally Kemp, 12 November, 2010
4 Alice Lowe, *Howard Luck Gossage: The Wizard of Ads* (Unpublished Biography), p.1
5 ibid, p.387
6 ibid, p.55
7 Interview with Jerry Mander, 14 March, 2011
8 Alice Lowe, p.344
9 Tom Wolfe, *Speech to Fordham University Graduate School of Arts and Sciences*, 25 February, 1999; Interview with Bob Scheer, 13 October, 2011
10 Stephen Fox, *The Mirror Makers: A History of American Advertising and its Creators* (New York, 1997; first published, New York, 1984), p.227
11 Kenneth Roman, *The King of Madison Avenue: David Ogilvy and the Making of Modern Advertising* (New York, 2009), p.4
12 Alice Lowe, p.347
13 Interview with Arthur Finger, 5 June, 2011
14 Alice Lowe, p.369
15 Interview with Alice Lowe, 16 November, 2010
16 Howard Luck Gossage, *Speech to the Art Directors' Club of Germany*, 5 November, 1966
17 Howard Luck Gossage, *Is There Any Hope for Advertising?*, edited by Kim Rotzell, Jarlath Graham, and Barrows Mussey (Chicago, 1986), p.xix
18 Alice Lowe, p.16
19 ibid, p.16

Chapter 2

1 Martin Mayer, *Madison Avenue U.S.A.* (London, 1961; first published, New York, 1958), p.152
2 *Advertising Age*, "Gossageisms: Sometimes Funny, Sometimes Poignant – Always Disturbingly Trenchant", 14 July, 1969
3 Letter from Howard Gossage to Barrows Mussey, 14 March, 1966
4 Alice Lowe, *Howard Luck Gossage: The Wizard of Ads* (Unpublished Biography), p.19
5 *Printers' Ink*, "They Write Ad Conversations", 5 August, 1960
6 Andrew Cracknell, *The Real Mad Men: The Remarkable True Story of Madison Avenue's Golden Era When a Handful of Renegades Changed Advertising For Ever* (London, 2011), pp.50–51
7 Interview with Jay Conrad Levinson, 31 October, 2010
8 *Direct*, "Legendary Copywriter Bill Jayme Dies at 75", 27 May, 2001

9 *The Kansas City Star*, "His Ads Are Crazy But Tinted Air Can Move Mountains", 2 February, 1964

10 Martin Mayer, p.19

11 ibid, p.23

12 Stephen Fox, *The Mirror Makers: A History of American Advertising and its Creators* (New York, 1997; first published, New York, 1984), p.209

13 Interview with Sally Kemp, 12 November, 2010

14 Interview with Alice Lowe, 21 May, 2011

15 Interview with Alice Lowe, 15 November, 2010

16 Interview with Dugald Stermer, 18 November, 2010

17 Interview with Sally Kemp, 13 November, 2010

18 Interview with Alice Lowe, 20 November, 2010

19 Alice Lowe, p.165

20 Letter from Howard Gossage to Barrows Mussey, 1 March , 1966

21 Howard Luck Gossage, *Is There Any Hope for Advertising?*, edited by Kim Rotzell, Jarlath Graham, and Barrows Mussey (Chicago, 1986), p.149

22 Interview with Sally Kemp, 12 November, 2010

23 Interview with Sally Kemp, 13 November, 2010

24 Jerry Della Femina, *From Those Wonderful Folks Who Gave You Pearl Harbor* (Edinburgh, 2010; first published, New York, 1970), pp.2–3

25 Jerry Mander, *Four Arguments for the Elimination of Television* (Goa, 1998; first published, New York, 1978), p.2

26 Alice Lowe, p.336

27 Interview with Sally Kemp, 13 November, 2010

28 Interview with Alice Lowe, 20 November, 2010

29 Interview with Jerry Mander, 17 November, 2010

30 Interview with Dugald Stermer, 18 November, 2010

31 Interview with Rich Silverstein, 15 November, 2010

32 Interview with Jay Conrad Levinson, 31 October, 2010

33 Alice Lowe pp.52–54

34 Martin Mayer, p.20

35 Interview with Jerry Mander, 17 November, 2010

36 Interview with Sally Kemp, 12 November, 2010

37 Tom Wolfe, *Speech of Remembrance: Howard Luck Gossage, Funeral Service*, 14 July, 1969

38 Alice Lowe, p.60

39 Interview with Sally Kemp, 12 November, 2010

40 Alice Lowe, p.2

41 Interview with Sally Kemp, 13 November, 2010

42 Herb Caen, *Speech of Remembrance: Howard Luck Gossage, Funeral Service*, 14 July, 1969

43 Interview with Dugald Stermer, 18 November, 2010

44 ibid

45 *Business Week*, "The Adman who Plays with Paper Airplanes", 11 February, 1967

46 Letter from Howard Gossage to Barrows Mussey, 28 March, 1967

47 Interview with Jeff Goodby, 15 March, 2011

48 *Advertising Age*, "Gossageisms: Sometimes Funny, Sometimes Poignant – Always Disturbingly Trenchant", 14 July, 1969

49 Alice Lowe, p.145

50 Interview with Dugald Stermer, 18 November, 2010

51 Martin Mayer, p.82

52 Interview with Sally Kemp, 13 November, 2010
53 Stephen Fox, p.258
54 Luke Sullivan, *"Hey Whipple, Squeeze This": A Guide to Creating Great Ads* (New York, 1998), p.227
55 Alice Lowe, p.144
56 Howard Luck Gossage, *Speech to the Art Directors' Club of Germany*, 5 November, 1966
57 Interview with Sally Kemp, 12 November, 2010

Chapter 3

1 Martin Mayer, *Madison Avenue U.S.A.* (London, 1961; first published, New York 1958), p.67
2 Stephen Fox, *The Mirror Makers: A History of American Advertising and its Creators* (New York, 1997; first published, New York, 1984), p.179
3 Interview with Professor Greg Pabst, 19 November, 2010
4 Jackie Merri Meyer (editor), *Mad Ave: Award-winning Advertising of the 20th Century* (New York, 2000), p.101
5 Rosser Reeves, *Reality in Advertising* (New York, 1990; first published, New York, 1961), pp.47–49
6 Martin Mayer, p.133
7 Stephen Fox, p.188
8 David Ogilvy, *The Unpublished David Ogilvy* (New York, 1986), p.135
9 Denis Higgins (editor), *The Art of Writing Advertising* (New York, 1965), p.108
10 ibid, p.107
11 Letter from Howard Gossage to Barrows Mussey, 3 September, 1965
12 Howard Gossage, *Speech to Sales Executive Club of New York*, 6 February, 1962
13 Larry Dobrow, *When Advertising Tried Harder. The Sixties: The Golden Age of American Advertising* (New York, 1984), p.22
14 Denis Higgins, p.97; p.109
15 Doris Willens, *Nobody's Perfect: Bill Bernbach and the Golden Age of Advertising* (2009), p.88
16 ibid, p. 17
17 David Ogilvy, p. 134
18 *Advertising Age*, "Gossage Tells Clinic Advertising is America's Only Original Art Form", 16 February, 1959
19 Letter from Howard Gossage to the president of *Printers' Ink*, 21 February, 1963
20 Letter from Howard Gossage to Barrows Mussey, 25 July, 1966
21 Alice Lowe, *The Wizard of Ads*, (Unpublished Biography), p.235
22 *Penn State Journal*, "How to Want to do Better Advertising", January 1963, p.1
23 Letter from Howard Gossage to Barrows Mussey, 3 September, 1965
24 *Advertising Age*, "Creativity Comes Best From 'Extra-Environmental Man' Not Stuck in Past, Says Gossage", 6 March, 1967
25 Alice Lowe, p.7
26 Flo Conway and Jim Siegelman, *Dark Hero of the Information Age: In Search of Norbert Wiener – The Father of Cybernetics* (New York, 2005), p.ix
27 Interview with James Harkin, 20 January, 2011
28 Conway and Siegelman, p.127
29 ibid, p.182
30 Interview with Professor Fred Turner, 19 November, 2010
31 Conway and Siegelman, p.185
32 ibid, p.251
33 *Time*, "The Push Button Cornucopia", 9 March, 1959

34 Interview with Professor Fred Turner, 19 November, 2010

35 Howard Gossage, *Speech to Sales Executive Club of New York*, 6 February, 1962.

36 *Advertising Age*, "Give Your Company a Clear, Consistent Identity and its Advertising will be Easier, Better: Gossage", 9 March, 1959

37 Howard Luck Gossage, *Speech to the Art Directors' Club of Germany*, 5 November, 1966

Chapter 4

1 Letter from Howard Gossage to Barrows Mussey, 3 September, 1965

2 Alice Lowe, *Howard Luck Gossage: The Wizard of Ads* (Unpublished Biography), p.249

3 Interview with Jeff Goodby, 15 March, 2011

4 Howard Luck Gossage, *Speech to the Art Directors' Club of Germany*, 5 November, 1966

5 Interview with Sally Kemp, 12 November, 2010

6 *The Kansas City Star*, "His Ads Are Crazy But Tinted Air Can Move Mountains", 2 February, 1964

7 Interview with Jerry Mander, 17 November, 2010

8 Lester Wunderman, *Being Direct: Making Advertising Pay* (New York, 2004; first published New York, 1996), p.126

9 Interview with Jeff Goodby, 15 March, 2011

10 Interview with Jerry Mander, 17 November, 2010

11 ibid

12 *Advertising Age*, "Give Your Company a Clear, Consistent Identity and its Advertising will be Easier, Better: Gossage", 9 March, 1959

13 Interview with Jerry Mander, 15 March, 2011

14 ibid

15 ibid

16 Howard Gossage, *Speech to Sales Executive Club of New York*, 6 February, 1962

17 Interview with Jerry Mander, 17 November, 2010

18 Interview with Dugald Stermer, 18 November, 2010

19 *Business Week*, "The Adman who Plays with Paper Airplanes", 11 February, 1967

20 Howard Luck Gossage, *Is There Any Hope for Advertising?*, edited by Kim Rotzell, Jarlath Graham, and Barrows Mussey (Chicago, 1986), p192

21 David Ogilvy, *An Autobiography* (London, 1997; first published, New York and London, 1978), p.118

22 Correspondence with Sally Kemp, 22 August, 2011

23 Martin Mayer, *Madison Avenue U.S.A.* (London, 1961; first published, New York, 1958), p.77

24 Alice Lowe, p.254

25 Ken Roman and Jane Maas, *How to Advertise: A Professional Guide for the Advertiser. What Works. What Doesn't. And Why* (New York, 1976), p.xi

26 *Advertising Age*, "Creativity Comes Best From 'Extra-Environmental Man' Not Stuck in Past, Says Gossage", 6 March, 1967

27 Alice Lowe, pp.63–64

28 ibid, pp. 73–74

29 Letter from Howard Gossage to Barrows Mussey, 11 September, 1966

30 Daniel J. Boorstin, *A Guide to Pseudo-Events in America* (New York, 1987; first published, New York, 1961), p.11

31 Letter from Howard Gossage to Barrows Mussey, 11 September, 1966

32 Interview with Jerry Mander, 17 November, 2010

33 Alice Lowe, p.108

34 ibid, p.110
35 ibid, p.116
36 Howard Luck Gossage, *Speech to the Art Directors' Club of Germany*, 5 November, 1966
37 Alice Lowe, p.120
38 ibid, p120
39 Interview with Rich Silverstein, 15 November, 2010
40 *The Kansas City Star*, "His Ads Are Crazy But Tinted Air Can Move Mountains", 2 February, 1964
41 *Business Week*, "The Adman who Plays with Paper Airplanes", 11 February, 1967
42 Alice Lowe, p.48
43 ibid, p.48
44 ibid, p.250
45 Interview with Jerry Mander, 17 November, 2010
46 Interview with Jeff Goodby, 15 March, 2011
47 *Ramparts*, "Understanding Marshall McLuhan", April, 1966
48 *Wired*, "The Wisdom of Saint Marshall, the Holy Fool", January, 1996

Chapter 5

1 Douglas Coupland, *Marshall McLuhan: You Know Nothing of My Work!* (New York, 2010), p.32
2 Alice Lowe, *Howard Luck Gossage: The Wizard of Ads* (Unpublished Biography), p.368
3 Fred Turner, *From Counterculture to Cyberculture: Stewart Brand, the Whole Earth Network and the Rise of Digital Utopianism* (Chicago, 2006), pp.52–53
4 James Harkin, *Cyburbia: The Dangerous Idea That's Changed How We Live and Who We Are* (London, 2009), pp.52–53
5 ibid, p.57
6 ibid, p.66
7 *The Bible: Authorised King James Version with Apocrypha* (Oxford and New York, 1998; first published Oxford and New York, 1997), p.201
8 Interview with Sally Kemp, 12 November, 2010
9 Interview with Jerry Mander, 17 November, 2010
10 Tom Wolfe "What If He Is Right?" in *The Pump House Gang* (New York, 1980; first published, New York, 1968), pp.113–114
11 ibid, p.113
12 Interview with Dugald Stermer, 18 November, 2010
13 *Business Week*, "The Adman who Plays with Paper Airplanes", 11 February, 1967
14 Tom Wolfe, p.113
15 Letter from Howard Gossage to Barrows Mussey, 3 September, 1965
16 Tom Wolfe, p.150
17 *Maclean's* "The High Priest of Pop Culture", 3 July, 1965; *Playboy*, "Marshall McLuhan: Mastermind", February, 1967; *Observer*, "The Electronic Prophet", 7 August, 1967
18 *Life*, "Oracle of the Electric Age", 25 February, 1966
19 Douglas Coupland, p.14; p.151
20 Interview with Alice Lowe, 15 November, 2010
21 Letter from Howard Gossage to Barrows Mussey, 30 January, 1966
22 ibid, 30 January, 1966
23 Bruce Bendinger, *The Book of Gossage* (Chicago, 1995), pp.41–42
24 *Advertising Age*, "Who Understands Media? Gossage Does; Explains All", 9 May, 1966
25 Bruce Bendinger, p.283

26 James Harkin, p.68

27 ibid, p.68

28 Dr. Hubert Burda, *The Digital Wunderkammer: 10 Chapters on the Iconic Turn* (Munich, 2011), p.178

29 Daniel J. Boorstin, A Guide to Pseudo-Events in America (New York, 1987; first published, New York, 1961), p. 57.

30 *Wired*, "The Wisdom of Saint Marshall, the Holy Fool", January, 1996

31 Interview with James Harkin, 20 January, 2011

32 ibid

33 Tom Wolfe, *Speech to Fordham University Graduate School of Arts and Sciences*, 25 February, 1999

34 *New Media Age*, "NMA Interview: Alex Bogusky", 22 February, 2007

35 Correspondence with Alex Bogusky, 7 September, 2011

36 Interview with Professor Greg Pabst, 19 November, 2010

37 Alice Lowe, p. 207

38 Interview with Professor Greg Pabst, 19 November, 2010

39 Interview with Sally Kemp, 13 November, 2010

40 Interview with Jeff Goodby, 15 March, 2011

41 Interview with Professor Fred Turner, 19 November, 2010

42 Interview with Professor Greg Pabst, 19 November, 2010

43 Interview with Alice Lowe, 20 November, 2010

44 Interview with Sally Kemp, 12 November, 2010

45 Interview with Jerry Mander, 14 March, 2011

Chapter 6

1 Interview with Kenneth Brower, 16 November, 2010

2 ibid

3 Michael P. Cohen, *The History of the Sierra Club: 1892–1970* (San Francisco, 1988), p.320

4 Interview with Tom Turner, 18 November, 2010

5 *Monumental: David Brower's Fight for Wild America*, Directed/Produced by Kelly Duane, Loteria Films, 2004

6 Correspondence with Jeff Ingram, 9 September, 2011

7 Interview with Jerry Mander, 17 November, 2010

8 Alice Lowe, *Howard Luck Gossage: The Wizard of Ads* (Unpublished Biography), p.333

9 Howard Luck Gossage, *Is There Any Hope for Advertising?*, edited by Kim Rotzell, Jarlath Graham, and Barrows Mussey (Chicago, 1986), p.184

10 Interview with Jerry Mander, 17 November, 2010

11 ibid

12 *Monumental: David Brower's Fight for Wild America*

13 Interview with Kenneth Brower, 16 November, 2010

14 Letter from Howard Gossage to Barrows Mussey, 11 September,1966

15 Morris Udall, *Congressional Record, Proceedings and Debates of 89th Congress, Second Session*, 9 June, 1966

16 *Monumental: David Brower's Fight for Wild America*

17 Interview with Tom Turner, 18 November, 2010

18 Interview with Jerry Mander, 17 November, 2010

19 *Monumental: David Brower's Fight for Wild America*

20 Interview with Jerry Mander, 17 November, 2010

21 Interview with Kenneth Brower, 16 November, 2010

22 A Message from the President, *The White House Conference on Natural Beauty*, Washington DC, May 24th–25th, 1965

23 Interview with Tom Turner, 18 November, 2010

24 Interview with Kenneth Brower, 16 November, 2010

25 Interview with Julia Butterfly Hill, 20 November, 2010

26 Jerry Mander, *Four Arguments for the Elimination of Television*, (Goa, 1998; first published, New York, 1978), p.8

27 Howard Luck Gossage, *Speech to the Art Directors' Club of Germany*, 5 November, 1966

28 Cohen, p.364

29 Interview with Kenneth Brower, 16 November, 2010

30 Jerry Mander, p.8

31 *Monumental: David Brower's Fight for Wild America*

32 Interview with Sally Kemp, 12 November, 2010

33 Correspondence with Tom Turner, 9 September, 2011

34 Interview with Jerry Mander, 17 November, 2010

35 Interview with Alice Lowe, 16 November, 2010

36 Interview Kenneth Brower, 16 November, 2010

37 ibid

38 *Monumental: David Brower's Fight for Wild America*

39 Interview with Kenneth Brower, 16 November, 2010

40 Howard Luck Gossage, *Ist Die Werbung Noch Zu Retten?*, edited by Kim Rotzell, Jarlath Graham, and Barrows Mussey (Dusseldorf, 1967)

Chapter 7

1 Stephen Fox, *The Mirror Makers: A History of American Advertising and its Creators* (New York, 1997; first published, New York, 1984), p.265

2 ibid, p.255; p.259

3 ibid, pp. 259–260

4 Interview with Jeff Goodby, 15 March, 2011

5 Interview with Bob McLaren, 22 November, 2011

6 Alice Lowe, *Howard Luck Gossage: The Wizard of Ads* (Unpublished Biography), p.1

7 Interview with Sally Kemp, 12 November, 2010

8 Letter from Howard Gossage to Barrows Mussey, 3 September, 1965

9 Interview with Sally Kemp, 12 November, 2010

10 Interview with Jerry Mander, 17 November, 2010

11 Interview with Professor Fred Turner, 19 November, 2010

12 Interview with Jerry Mander, 17 November, 2010

13 Interview with Sally Kemp, 13 November, 2010

14 Interview with Professor Fred Turner, 19 November, 2010

15 Interview with Bob Scheer, 13 October, 2011

16 Interview with Dagmar Mussey, 27 April, 2011

17 Correspondence with Sally Kemp, 29 April, 2011

18 Letter from Howard Gossage to Barrows Mussey, 27 April, 1967

19 Letter from Howard Gossage to Barrows Mussey, 11 January, 1968

20 Interview with Jerry Mander, 17 November, 2010

21 Interview with Alice Lowe, 15 November, 2010

22 Interview with Jerry Mander, 17 November, 2010

23 ibid

24 Interview with Jerry Mander, 14 March, 2011

25 Alice Lowe, p.427

26 David Ogilvy, *Ogilvy on Advertising* (New York 1985; first published, London and New York, 1983), p.152

27 Interview with Arthur Finger, 5 June, 2011

28 *Scanlan's* "The Log of the Anguilla Free Trade Charter Company", April, 1970

29 ibid

30 Howard Luck Gossage, *Is There Any Hope for Advertising?*, edited by Kim Rotzell, Jarlath Graham, and Barrows Mussey (Chicago, 1986), p.197

31 Letter from Howard Gossage to Barrows Mussey, 28 June, 1967

32 Letter from Howard Gossage to Barrows Mussey, 5 August, 1968

33 *Advertising Age*, "If You're Stuck with a Lemon, Make Lemonade, Says Undaunted Gossage", 3 February, 1969

34 ibid

Chapter 8

1 Alice Lowe, *Howard Luck Gossage: The Wizard of Ads* (Unpublished Biography), p.8

2 Interview with Bob McLaren, 22 October, 2011

3 Interview with Dugald Stermer, 18 November, 2010

4 Alice Lowe, p. 398

5 Interview with Bob McLaren, 22 October, 2011

6 Warren Hinckle, *Speech of Remembrance: Howard Luck Gossage, Funeral Service*, 14 July, 1969

7 Interview with Jerry Mander, 15 March, 2011

8 Letter from Howard Gossage to Barrows Mussey, 5 April, 1969

9 Letter from Howard Gossage to Barrows Mussey, 30 December, 1968

10 Letter from Howard Gossage to Barrows Mussey, 5 April, 1969

11 Letter from Howard Gossage to Barrows Mussey, 8 March, 1968

12 Tom Wolfe, "The Man Who Always Peaked Too Soon", in *Mauve Gloves & Madmen, Clutter & Vine*, (First published, New York, 1976; New York, 1977), pp.12–23

13 Letter from Howard Gossage to Barrows Mussey, 22 November, 1968

14 ibid

15 ibid

16 Alice Lowe, p.280

17 *Advertising Age*, "Advertising Has Tremendous (Unwanted) Economic Power and Here Are Things It Should Do About It", 5 May, 1969

18 ibid

19 *Advertising Age*, "Improve Media: Gossage to Admen", 9 May, 1966

20 *Advertising Age*, "Advertising Has Tremendous (Unwanted) Economic Power and Here Are Things It Should Do About It"

21 Alice Lowe, p.403

22 ibid, pp.412–413

23 ibid, p.414

24 Interview with Alice Lowe, 20 November, 2010

25 Stephen Fox, *The Mirror Makers: A History of American Advertising and its Creators* (New York, 1997; first published, New York, 1984), p.271

26 ibid, p.261

27 Interview with Alice Lowe, 15 November, 2010

28 Interview with Jeff Goodby, 15 March, 2011

29 ibid

30 Interview with Rich Silverstein, 15 November, 2010

31 Correspondence with Rory Sutherland, 12 November, 2011

32 Interview with Jeff Goodby 15 March, 2011

33 Andrew Cracknell, *The Real Mad Men: The Remarkable True Story of Madison Avenue's Golden Era When a Handful of Renegades Changed Advertising For Ever* (London, 2011), p.64

34 Interview with Jeff Goodby, 15 March, 2011

35 Warren Hinckle, *Speech of Remembrance: Howard Luck Gossage, Funeral Service*

36 Alice Lowe, pp.139–140

37 Interview with Sally Kemp, 13 November, 2010

38 Howard Luck Gossage, *Is There Any Hope for Advertising?*, edited by Kim Rotzell, Jarlath Graham, and Barrows Mussey (Chicago, 1986), p.xv

39 Interview with Sally Kemp, 12 November, 2010

40 Interview with Dugald Stermer, 18 November, 2010

41 ibid

42 Interview with Bob Scheer, 13 November, 2011

43 ibid

44 Interview with Jay Conrad Levinson, 31 October, 2010

45 ibid

46 Interview with Jeff Goodby, 15 March, 2011

47 Correspondence with Alex Bogusky, 7 September, 2011

48 Interview with Dr. Hubert Burda, 4 May, 2011

49 ibid

50 ibid

51 Tom Wolfe, *Speech of Remembrance: Howard Luck Gossage, Funeral Service*, 14 July, 1969

52 Alice Lowe, p.439

53 Interview with Dugald Stermer, November 18, 2010

INDEX

About the author

Steve Harrison got his PhD with his thesis: *American Society, Cinema and Television, 1950–60*. He then became a trainee copywriter at 30. Thereafter he was a european creative director and global creative director either side of starting, and then selling, his own agency. Until retiring from agency life in 2007, he won more Cannes Lions Awards than any other creative director in his discipline; and in 2009 explained all in his book *How to do better creative work*. Like Howard Luck Gossage, he always encouraged people to respond to his work, and would be delighted if you'd email him on harrisosteve@googlemail.com and let him know what you think about this book.